AF248711

# InSights

# InSights

## Observations
## from Paris

*Revised Edition*

Carol L. Couch

MADWOMAN PRESS
NEW MEXICO

ISBN 978-1-7357555-3-3
Library of Congress Control Number: 2024900634

Madwoman Press
Santa Fe, NM
USA

Printed in the United States of America
at Gorham Printing, Inc.

Cover and book design: Joan Julian

For Les<br>because we will never have Paris

# CONTENTS

## PART II: LA GRANDE EXPÉDITION

# Preface to the Original Edition

This set of musings began as a cliché. A romantic fantasy. Paris.

The romance was with writing. The fantasy was that I could write something if only I sat long enough over a café crème in one of Paris's historic literary cafés. During my early trips, I would sometimes send emails to family and friends, attaching photos and observations about what I had seen and thought. That was, perhaps, a start.

My 2020 trip was to be my longest yet, which caused a few complications. Because I was staying for three months, the apartments were governed by bail mobilité, a type of lease that applies to furnished apartments let between one and ten months.

Because the bail mobilité is limited to people who are staying for work or study, I needed some sort of documentation to that effect. Just something to fulfill a legal technicality that didn't need to be too tethered to reality. My student days being long past, the best fit in the approved list of categories was for a "temporary assignment as part of a professional activity." But what professional activity and on assignment for whom?

To satisfy the latter, I asked my sister Joan, as proprietor of Insights + Strategy by Design, if she would sign a letter saying I was on temporary assignment for her. Her work involved creative collaboration with multidisciplinary teams. Surely, I could make up some faux temporary assignment that would appear to tie in with that.

As for the professional activity, it just had to be specific enough to be plausible. Taking a cue from Joan's business' name, maybe it could have something to do with insights? Sights that prompted . . . insights? I could pretend to be writing . . . something. . .?

That something eventually became this book.

This book, therefore, is the outgrowth of a legal formality, conceived as a fiction. A fiction that led to the fulfillment of a romantic fantasy.

January 2021
Santa Fe NM

# Preface to the Revised Edition

The first edition of this book was written as a lark, primarily as a way of sharing my travels and thoughts with family and friends.

In this revised edition, the material has been edited in several ways.

First and foremost, some errors have been corrected. Some, undoubtedly, remain.

Secondly, some of the material in the first edition has been removed because its interest was solely personal. In the same vein, some of the text and images have changed to improve readability.

Thirdly, entries have been updated when relevant.

And, so, here it is.


July 2024
Santa Fe NM

# Maps

United Kingdom
Belgium
Germany
Luxembourg
Paris
FRANCE
Switzerland
Italy
Spain

17
18
19
Sacré-Cœur
9
8
10
2
20
16
1
Louvre
7
3
Eiffel Tower
11
Père Lachaise
4
Notre Dame
6
5
12
15
Seine River
14
13
Hippodrome
Vincennes
Versailles

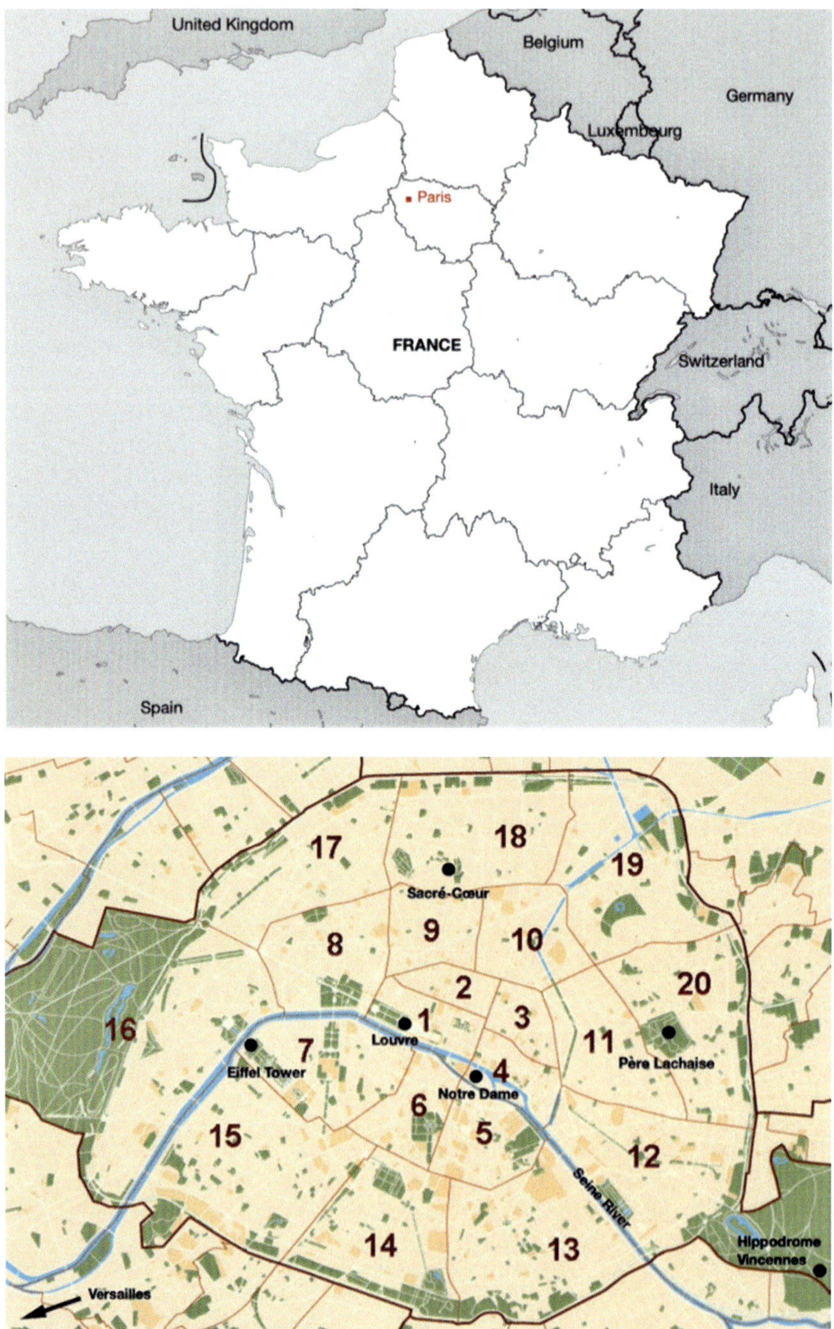

# PART I
## Early Trips - Paris

---

2007

2010

2012

2018

# Paris

July 2 to July 31, 2007

## 24 rue de la Rochefoucauld, 9th arr.
Métro: Trinité (Line 12)

It was shocking. I overheard two guys in church tell the minister that they were renting an apartment in Paris for two months. An apartment? In Paris? Two *months*? A new world opened up, the world of VRBO, Vacation Rental By Owner. A world where one really could rent an apartment in Paris for two months. Dorothy might long to go over the rainbow. I was going to Paris.

I knew I wanted a classic Parisian place to stay. I didn't worry overmuch about what "classic" meant in the grand scheme of Parisian history. For me, it was Haussmann-style elegance.

After scouring online options, I found a gem in the non-touristy 9th arrondissement on the Right Bank of the Seine. I booked it by signing a simple contract over the internet after setting up a PayPal account to transfer the deposit. It was shockingly simple. Friends and family planned to join me at different times during that first magical trip. Paris! Dreams really do come true.

Looking out from our apartment window (opposite page)

## The Métro

It's old. It's big. It's dense. It's busy. It's efficient. It's beautiful. It's civilized. It's one of my favorite things about Paris.

It is also entertaining.

Performances start daily at 5:30 a.m. and run continuously until after midnight. The stage set includes more than 300 stations, 130 miles of track and over 21,400 directional signs. Season passes are available.

There is a cast of millions. Over four million on an average day. It has had an exceptionally long run, having opened in 1900.

It is mostly improvisation, although the métro map does provide some structural guidance. The spontaneity and fluidity of movement is the métro's defining quality.

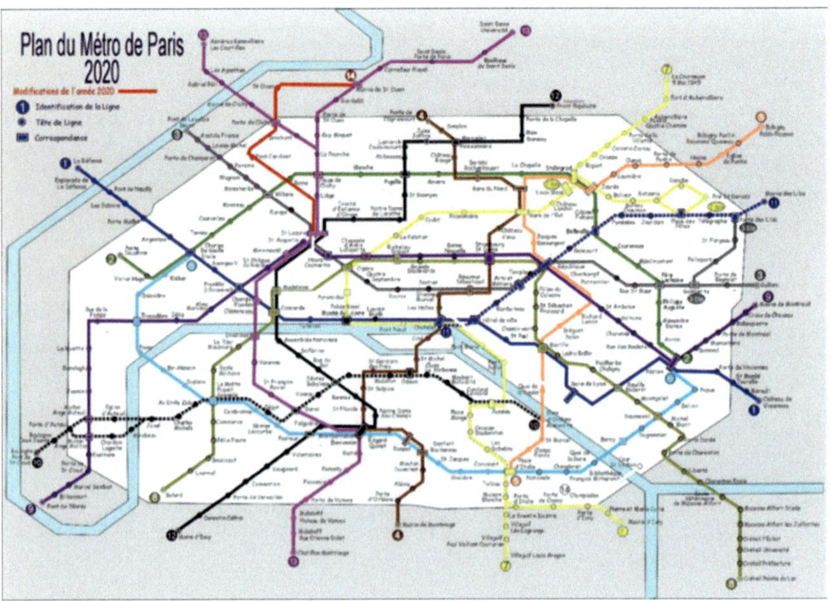

METRO
Glacier
Café
SAINT-MICHEL

There are different types of métro cars along its sixteen lines. The cars enter the station with a soft rumble and bright light, turning a dark corner before easing to a smooth stop. Platform signs announce the direction of the line and flash the wait times until the next train, rarely more than four minutes away.

Stationary seats within the cars are effortlessly filled and emptied as the performers slip sideways around knees and packages. Those sitting on the fold down seats near the doors unobtrusively stand when an unspoken but intuitively acknowledged density is reached.

There are automatic doors, push button doors, and lever doors. On the platforms, there are benches to sit on, horizontal bars to lean against, and molded plastic chairs connected in groups of four or more. There are stairs and escalators and elevators. There are labyrinths of tunnels and platforms. Everywhere there are ads. Commercial ads, poetry ads, public service ads.

The cast sport all manner of costumes. Makeup is minimal. Props include strollers, shopping bags, briefcases, books, newspapers, folding maps, guidebooks, luggage and, recently, cellphones.

Someone plays an accordion or amplified violin then walks the length of the car holding out a cup with a beckoning look and a "Merci, madame, monsieur." Regular commuters look away. Tourists may drop in a coin.

As the train nears a stop, one hears "pardon" whispered as passengers deftly maneuver toward the door to exit. Bodies subtly shift as people accommodate the influx and outflow. Never a push or shove. Never a sharp movement or angry glare. There are some discrete, appraising looks, checking one another out. Sometimes, rarely, a smile between strangers as they catch a quick glance at a shared amusement. There are also slumped figures hunched into their seats, seeking refuge from economic despair.

Tourists, businessmen, students, parents, children, workers, shoppers, the unhoused, and lovers - all are characters to be found on the métro.

I'm reminded of the lyrics from the song *La même histoire* (The same story):

*Life is a dance we all have to do*
*What does the music require?*
*People are moving together*
*Close as the flames in a fire.*

*Feel the beat,*
*Music, and rhyme*
*While there is time.*

*We all go round and round*
*Partners are lost and found*
*Looking for one more chance.*
*All I know is*
*We're all in the dance.*

METROPOLITAIN
ABBESSES

# Des Lignes et des Rimes
## (The Lines and the Rhymes)

Since 1997, RATP, the state-owned public transportation company for the Paris region, has tucked little gems of poetry in amongst the cacophony of advertising. A sigh of literature amongst the shouts of commercialization.

*Where are the children?*
*In the attic*
*Full of gold and spiders*
*Hidden in their costumes*
*To fool the moon.*

*Poetry without answer -*
*ocean without end*
*it is drowning*
*in a seashell*

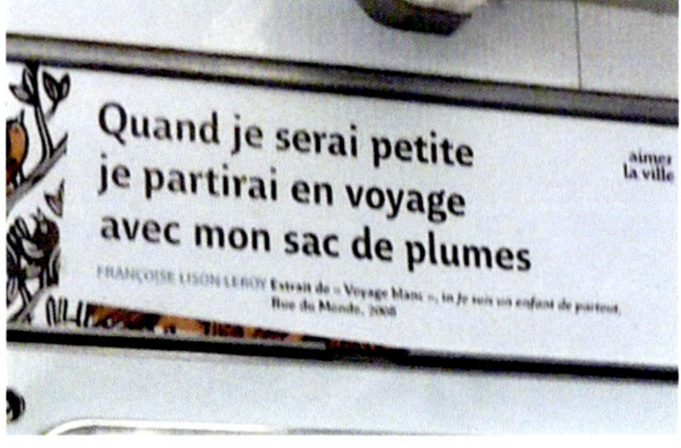


*When I am little*
*I'll go on a trip*
*with my bag of feathers*

Un bel oiseau me montre la lumière
Elle est dans ses yeux, bien en vue,
Il chante sur une boule de gui
Au milieu du soleil.
A beautiful bird shows me the light
It's in her eyes, in plain sight
She sings on a ball of mistletoe
In the middle of the sun
Les maths ?
Une équation bientôt résolue !
0 800 405
www.unepiece.com
BESOIN DE PLACE POUR VOS ARCHIVES ?
une pièce en plus
A LOUER POUR TOUT RANGER
Le N°1 du Self-Stockage à Paris
Boxes individuels de stockage de 1m² à 100m²
PARKING GRATUIT
onoff
Ma de pro
Votre secon avec u
Seconde ligne
Protégez votre vie privée

## What Do We Remember?

We cannot remember what we do not know.

Sitting in Hotel Lutetia's bar, I wondered whether buildings have memories. It opened in 1910 and, within a decade, Russian exiles from the 1917 revolution made it their home. During WWI, the Red Cross was

The Hotel Lutetia in the 6th arrondissement on the Left Bank. Charles and Yvonne de Gaulle spent their honeymoon here in 1921.

headquartered there and guest rooms were given to the injured. In the late 1930s, Germans, mostly Jewish, came to stay. Anti-Nazi exiles including Heinrich Mann, brother of the novelist Thomas, and Willie Brandt, later chancellor of Germany, would meet in the bar.

When the Germans occupied Paris in June 1940, however, it was requisitioned by the Abwehr, a counter-intelligence unit of the German army. (Not to be confused with the Gestapo.)

When Paris was liberated in August 1944, it became a reparations center for prisoners of war, displaced persons, and survivors of concentration camps. In 1955, it was acquired by the Tattinger family who made their fortune in champagne. Now, it is owned by the Israeli Alrov group.

The Alrov group is not anxious to remind guests about the troubled history of its hotel. Only a small plaque on the façade, high above eye level, commemorates the hotel's role, for good and evil, in WWII and its aftermath.

Others, throughout Paris, have tried to ensure that we don't forget both the shameful and heroic history of Paris in WWII. Dozens of plaques and memorials are affixed to buildings or erected in parks to commemorate those who were deported and killed.

Place de la Concorde, August 26, 1944
Crowds of Parisians, who were celebrating the entry of Allied
troops into Paris, scatter for cover from German sniper fire.

I sought out the Victor Hugo school in the Marais, an historically Jewish neighborhood, where 500 children were rounded up and killed in concentrations camps. The plaque at the entrance reads:

> From 1942 to 1944, over 11,000 children were deported
> from France by the Nazis with the active participation of the
> Vichy government and murdered in the death camps because
> they were Jews. More than 500 of these children lived in the
> 3rd arrondissement and went to Victor Hugo School.

Still in use today, all I could do was stand in front of the oversized entrance, imagining little ones walking out the door for the last time, perhaps laughing or shouting at the freedom from classes at the end of a school day, not knowing what awaited them. I thought of today's students who walk in and out of that same door. What must they remember?

A memorial in Square Boucicaut between Le Bon Marché and Hotel Lutetia. The inscription translates to:

*Arrested by the police of the Vichy Government, in collaboration with the Nazis, 11,000 children were deported from France between 1942 and 1944 and murdered in Auschwitz because they were Jews.*

*Many lived in the 7th arrondissement, among them two little ones who didn't have time to go to school.*

*Passing by, read their names.*
*Your memory is their only grave.*

*Sarah Azaria, 5 years*
*Félicie Lanz, 4 years*

*Let us never forget them.*

I also went to the combined Musée Jean Moulin, Musée de Libération de Paris, and the Musée du Général Leclerc in the 14th arrondissement. Moulin unified the various factions of the French Resistance. Leclerc formed the 2nd Armored Division, which, along with US forces and civilian resisters, liberated Paris in August 1944.

It is a brilliantly curated museum complex. Its itinerary provides a chronological history of Paris from the end of the First World War to the mass exodus of Parisians as the Germans approached in 1940, through the Nazi occupation to the Paris insurrection that began on August 8th through the liberation of Paris and its complex aftermath.

A row of memorial plaques along Rue Rivoli next to the Place de Concorde, commemorating those who died for the liberation of Paris in August 1944

There is so much more to know. Lifetimes of information to learn. For those interested, I would recommend these books as at least a starting point:

Marc Bloch, *Strange Defeat: A Statement of Evidence Written in 1940* (1999)

Peter Hayes, *Why? Explaining the Holocaust* (2017)

Agnès Humbert, *Resistance: A Woman's Journal of Struggle and Defiance in Occupied France* (2008) [first published in France in 1946]

Don and Petie Kladstrup, *Wine & War: The French, the Nazis, and the Battle for France's Greatest Treasure* (2001)

Damien Lewis, *Agent Josephine: American Beauty, French Hero, British Spy* (2022)

Jacques Lusseyran, *And There Was Light: The Extraordinary Memoir of a Blind Hero of the French Resistance in World War II* (2014)

Caroline Moorehead, *A Train in Winter: An Extraordinary Story of Women, Friendship, and Resistance in Occupied France* (2012)

Irène Némirovsky, *Suite Française* (2006)

Robert O. Paxton, *Vichy France: Old Guard and New Order, 1940-1944* (2001)

Richard Vinen, *The Unfree French: Life Under the Occupation* (2006)

Victims and heroes. Let us not forget.

## Notre Dame de Paris

*This section is based on my 2007 experience of visiting Notre Dame Cathedral. My experience of the Cathedral after the devastating fire on April 15, 2019, is included in Part II.*

My Catholic upbringing did not school me in transepts or ambulatories or clerestories or apses or parvises or, God help me, tympanum or trumeau. I have never had a good grasp of the distinction between the Romanesque and Gothic. And the sheer number of sculptures here, there, and everywhere in and around the cathedral are mind-numbing.

I tried to learn a few things besides the fact that Notre Dame is the most visited monument in France with tens of thousands of visitors a day. That was kinda obvious from the crowds.

Construction began around 1163 during the reign of Louis VII. It was officially completed in 1345 during the reign of Philip VI. The use of flying buttresses was a pioneering technology, allowing for higher and thinner walls with larger windows because the buttresses relieved the walls of bearing all the weight of the roof.

The cathedral was seized during the French Revolution and dedicated to the Cult of Reason in 1793. Napoleon returned the cathedral to the Catholic Church in 1802 and subsequently crowned himself Emperor there in 1804. Victor Hugo wrote his 1831 novel *The Hunchback of Notre Dame* to save the cathedral from demolition after it fell into disrepair during the Napoleonic Wars.

I wish now that I had read Allan Temko's *Notre Dame de Paris* before I went to see it. The book reads like a biography rather than a textbook and, although there are still far too many sculptures and architectural details to absorb, Temko's book gives the cathedral a life and context worth understanding.

What I understood as a tourist in 2007 was that the lines were long, the interior was dark and cold, and it felt cavernously claustrophobic.

Fortunately, I experienced Notre Dame as a congregant as well as a tourist. On the Sunday my sister Jeanne was in Paris, we decided to attend an early Mass there. We set our alarms and rode an empty métro to the empty expanse in front of the cathedral.

Being alone together in front of the massive western façade and attending Mass allowed us the opportunity to experience Notre Dame more intimately as a place for spiritual, not just architectural, worship.

After Mass, we turned our attention to the more secular attractions of Notre Dame and went outside to get in the line to ascend the towers.

The thing about towers is that they tend to be tall and have quite a lot of steps to get the top. Four hundred and twenty-two steps in the case of Notre Dame's towers – or so I'm told. The actual number of steps wasn't so much a problem as the dizzyingly tight turns. Only with Jeanne's gentle coaxing was I able to keep moving. Just take it slow and don't look down.

Looking up – good

Looking down – bad

At some point stone steps gave way to timber and we found ourselves in an ancient hewn forest, winding our way heavenward.

Lit up in the dark was the bell. The Great Bell, Le Grand Bourdon, christened Emmanuel Louis Thérése. All of the religious bells in Notre Dame are baptized. Guillaume, Gabriel, Claude, Marie, Jacqueline, Françoise, and Barbara, among others, have all rung out from within its towers and under its spire. Emmanuel, weighing in at almost 30,000 pounds, is the only bell to have survived the French Revolution when all the other bells were recast for cannon.

A few more steps and we were out in the sunshine. We had gone as high as we could go.

It was pretty high. We were among the first allowed up the towers and our guide and escort, seeing how reluctant Jeanne and I were to leave, told us that we could stay longer and go back down with the next group. The views were so spectacular we could have stayed up there for hours.

From the sublime to the grotesque, Notre Dame, Our Lady, had truly blessed this day.

　　　　The "forest" supporting Notre Dame's roof

Emmanuel

Notre Dame's spire and the Seine

Grotesques & gargoyles

Note: Gargoyles (figures at the end of waterspouts) should be distinguished from chimeras and grotesques (fantastical creatures used for decorative purposes). Take note, trivia players.

Gargoyles

A rain spout without a gargoyle

# Père Lachaise Cemetery

Why do we visit the remains of the dead? In the case of Père Lachaise, it may be to get away from the city's crowds and stroll its cool, tree-lined walks.

If you go, you will walk amongst many notable personages. And many more known but to God.

Among the monuments to the unnamed dead are more than a dozen commemorating those in died in concentration camps during WWII and those who fought in the Resistance. Another monument, the Mur des Fédérés, marks the communal grave at the spot where 146 insurgents were shot during the Paris Commune of 1870. There is an ossuary, Monument aux Morts, where the bones and cremated remains of unidentified Parisians are kept. An inscription on that monument, as translated into English, reads, "For those who live in the shadow of darkness, the light shines."

Of the great and good – or at least great, one hesitates to pass judgment on their goodness – are Oscar Wilde, Chopin, Balzac, Colette, Marcel Marceau, Seurat, Bizet, Delacroix, Jacques-Louis David, Ingres, Modigliani, Pissarro, Sarah Bernhardt, Isadora Duncan, Escoffier, Gertrude Stein, Alice B. Toklas, Jane Avril, Jean de Brunhoff, Caillebotte, Honoré Daumier, Stéphane Grappelli, Jean Moulin, and Richard Wright. As I walked around and between the gravestones, I couldn't help but wonder what so many writers, painters, performers, musicians, and even a chef and WWII Resistance leader, might say to one another after the cemetery closes and their ghosts wander among the graves.

Not all are left to rest in peace. Especially not Jim Morrison, the lead singer for The Doors. His grave was initially unmarked but fans found it and turned it into a prime party spot. The surrounding graves were vandalized.

A classic grotesque (opposite page)

Empty liquor bottles, drug paraphernalia, and trash were strewn about. A concrete liner was placed around Morrison's grave for protection. Fans chipped off pieces as souvenirs. A bust of Morrison was installed by an admirer, repeatedly defaced, and finally stolen.

On the twentieth anniversary of his death, in 1991, his parents, from whom he had been estranged long before his death, came to Paris for a kind of reconciliation. The space was cleaned up and a new headstone installed. The inscription, chosen by his father, a retired admiral, reads:

James Douglas Morrison
1943 - 1971
KATA TON ΔAIMONA EAYTOY

The literal translation is "According to his own daimon" but it is often interpreted as "True to his own spirit."

Jim Morrison's grave

When I visited in 2007, the grave was sectioned off by a fence and only elaborate flower arrangements were left in tribute. The liquor bottles and rough partying may have been more in keeping with how he lived his life, but I like to think the flowers reflect the poetry and peace he hoped to find in moving to Paris.

The most popular graves, including Jim Morrison's, are marked on a map thoughtfully provided by the cemetery, though I recommend buying the more readable and complete maps independently sold at the entrances for a euro or two. At 110 acres, the largest cemetery in Paris, there is a lot of ground to cover.

Not only is Père Lachaise large, it is said to be the most visited cemetery in the world with over 3.5 million visitors annually.

It didn't used to be so popular. When it first opened in 1804, the cemetery only had thirteen graves. Being far from the city center and the grounds not being blessed by the Catholic Church, few were interested in spending eternity there.

What it needed was celebrity appeal. The owners managed to transfer the remains of Jean de La Fontaine and Molière to the cemetery. That helped a little. Burials gradually increased but, still, there were only 833 gravesites in 1812. Then, Abélard's and Hélöise's remains were transferred to the cemetery.

That got the ball rolling. Burials dramatically increased so that, by 1830, the cemetery housed the remains of over 33,000 souls. Today, two to three million remains are interred at Père Lachaise, including those in the ossuary.

New burials are being accepted, although there is a waiting list. In the rare instance a plot becomes available, you may buy it in perpetuity or lease it for ten, thirty, or fifty years. As with all prime real estate, leases are strictly enforced. If your lease expires, expect to be evicted to the ossuary.

The cheapest way to get into Père Lachaise is to be alive. There is no entrance fee for visitors.

# **Paris**

March 23 to April 23, 2010

# 6 rue St. Lazare, 9th arr.
## Métro: Notre Dame de Lorette (Line 12)

Like so many before me, I willingly succumbed to Paris' charms. Three years after my first trip, I returned for another month's stay in the same neighborhood but in a different apartment. Still in a Haussmann building, still with a certain elegance and all the practicalities an apartment offered, still with friends and family visiting, and still able to pretend in delusional moments that I was living an authentic Parisian life.

Entrance to 6 rue St. Lazare

# A Failed Flâneuse

There is a particular, one might say peculiar, Parisian personality - the flâneur. Or flâneuse, if one is a woman.

Flâneur has no equivalent in the English language. Various translations suggest loafer, idler, saunterer, or even loiterer. But all of these miss the essence of the flâneur. A flâneur observes life as he leisurely strolls without purpose or plan. A flâneur is a connoisseur of the boulevards. While wandering aimlessly, the flâneur nevertheless takes note of everything he encounters. Not for any particular purpose, but only for pleasure.

People from the United States don't make particularly good flâneurs. We have too much to do. We are people of action, productivity, self-improvement. The flâneur is in search of experiences, pure, raw . . . and useless. Americans want to know something or learn something. We must have a purpose. In the United States, the sidewalk is an anonymous conveyer belt. In Paris, it is a stage.

Personally, I am predisposed to sauntering rather than walking. I rather like the idea of observing life while meandering about. I thought I might try to become a flâneuse on this trip.

It is not as easy as it seems.

One cloudy day, I had nothing in particular to do. "Ah!," I thought, "a good day to test my mettle as a flâneuse." (But, you see, already I had the wrong attitude. Testing mettle? No, no, no.) So, with a deep breath of determination (determination? No!), I adjusted my attitude and nonchalantly suggested to myself that I might stroll in the general direction of Sacré-Cœur. I neglected to consider that Sacré-Cœur sits on the top of Montmartre, the Mount of the Martyr. Yes, uphill. Sometimes steeply uphill. Nevertheless, off I went and, with a bit of huff and puff, reached the summit. My reward was a stunning panoramic view of Paris. It was worth the effort.

Dang it. There I go again. Reward? Effort? Aimlessness seeks no reward. Effort is not to be measured. This sauntering flâneuse stuff took a lot of discipline. I soldiered on. Well, I tried not soldier. Saunter. Saunter. Saunter.

Sacré-Cœur

View from Sacré-Cœur

From Sacré-Cœur, there was nowhere to go but down. Better for sauntering, yes? Well, yes. Except for the hordes of tourists who had thronged to the streets. One may shuffle through a crowd. One can hardly saunter. And observations are generally limited to whoever or whatever one is about to walk into.

 Along rue Steinkerque

Finally, away from the crowds, I was able to recover a more leisurely pace as I strolled west through Montmartre to Les Deux Moulins, the café where they filmed *Amelie*. A quiet lunch, lingering over a café creme, seemed just the ticket to reset my flâneuse-ness. But the morning had left me agitated. I got up and slipped away before the waiter came for my order.

With no thought but to stop for some groceries on the way home, I began to walk (I no longer cared if it was a saunter or a forced march), down rue de Notre Dame de Lorette. Caring not a wit that I had a defined purpose with a specific destination, I managed to be thwarted even in this. The grocery I was looking for was not to be found. I later discovered I was on the wrong street. Home, however, was ultimately achieved.

I regrouped back at the apartment. It was barely afternoon. I decided to venture out again. By now, I had given up on my ambition to become a flâneuse. I would embrace my cultural heritage of purposeful determination. I gave up meandering, briskly walked out the front door of my apartment, and took the most efficient route to the métro. My explicit goal was WHSmith, "The Largest English Bookshop in Paris since 1903."

What can I say? We are who we are.

Les Deux Moulins, 15 rue Lepic

Soon enough, there I was, at WHSmith. Searching in the history section, I found exactly the book I was looking for, *Liberation, the Bitter Road to Freedom, Europe 1944-1945.* In a lighter vein, I also picked up The *Widow Clicquot: The Story of a Champagne Empire and the Woman Who Ruled It.* Inspired by the Widow Clicquot and sighing with the satisfaction of a job well done, I bought champagne on the way home.

Maybe, someday, if I spend enough time in Paris, I will become a proper flâneuse.

In the meantime, I'll pop open my champagne, rest from a day of too much walking, and settle down with a good book.

# La Légende des Cloches de Pâques
(The Legend of the Easter Bells)

While staying at 6 rue St. Lazare, church bells from the nearby Notre Dame de Lorette church would chime reassuringly every fifteen minutes. But not every day. Over Eastertide, church bells throughout France fall silent during Holy Week in mourning for Christ's suffering and death.

There is also a child-friendly legend of the Easter bells. In this telling, the bells fall silent because they have flown away to Rome to be blessed by the Pope and to collect treats for the children. They fly back Easter morning and ring out joyously to announce that Easter has arrived.

The bells of Notre Dame de Lorette did return on Easter and chimed and chimed all morning. To share in the magic of the children's legend, I bought treats for myself and friends. I thanked the bells.

## A Study in Contrasts

In 2007, the city was plastered with Disney advertisements for *Ratatouille*, which featured a rat, Rémy, who was a brilliant chef and the hero of the story. Next to him was his brother, Émile, a good-hearted fellow who was happy to eat anything and everything. He was a rat d'égout, a sewer rat. Rémy was a rat de goût, a gourmet rat. They offered a study in contrasts.

Gourmet rat                                                    Sewer rat

In 2010, my friends, Gina and Lynn, and I decided to breakfast at the Ritz in their two star Michelin restaurant, La Table de L'Espadon. Perhaps retaining a subliminal message from the 2007 ads, my brain latched on to the idea of visiting Paris's sewer museum afterward. De goût and d'egout.

It is perhaps not surprising that the sewer museum, Musée des Égouts de Paris, is one of the less frequented museums in Paris. An unobtrusive ticket booth serves as its entrance, hidden along the Quai d'Orsay near the Pont de l'Alma.

Paris's sewers have welcomed tourists since the Exposition Universelle in 1867. Originally, tours were given in locomotive wagons. Then, until the 1970s, tourists sat in boats pulled by sewer workers. Today, tourists are on foot, taking self-guided tours along raised walkways above the working sewer canals. It doesn't smell as bad as this may imply. Some guidebooks suggest bringing along a scented handkerchief. I got along fine without one.

La Table de L'Espadon at the Ritz

A postcard for the Musée des Égouts de Paris

SAUF

The brochure for the self-guided tour emphatically states in English:

*WARNING!*

*In this operating site, it is important to comply to the following security and hygiene instructions:*

- *Avoid any contact with wastewater, walls, pipes,*
- *do not eat,*
- *wash your hands when you exit,*
- *do not run, do not bend over the manrope…*

*For their security, do not forget to inform the children under your responsibility about those security rules.*

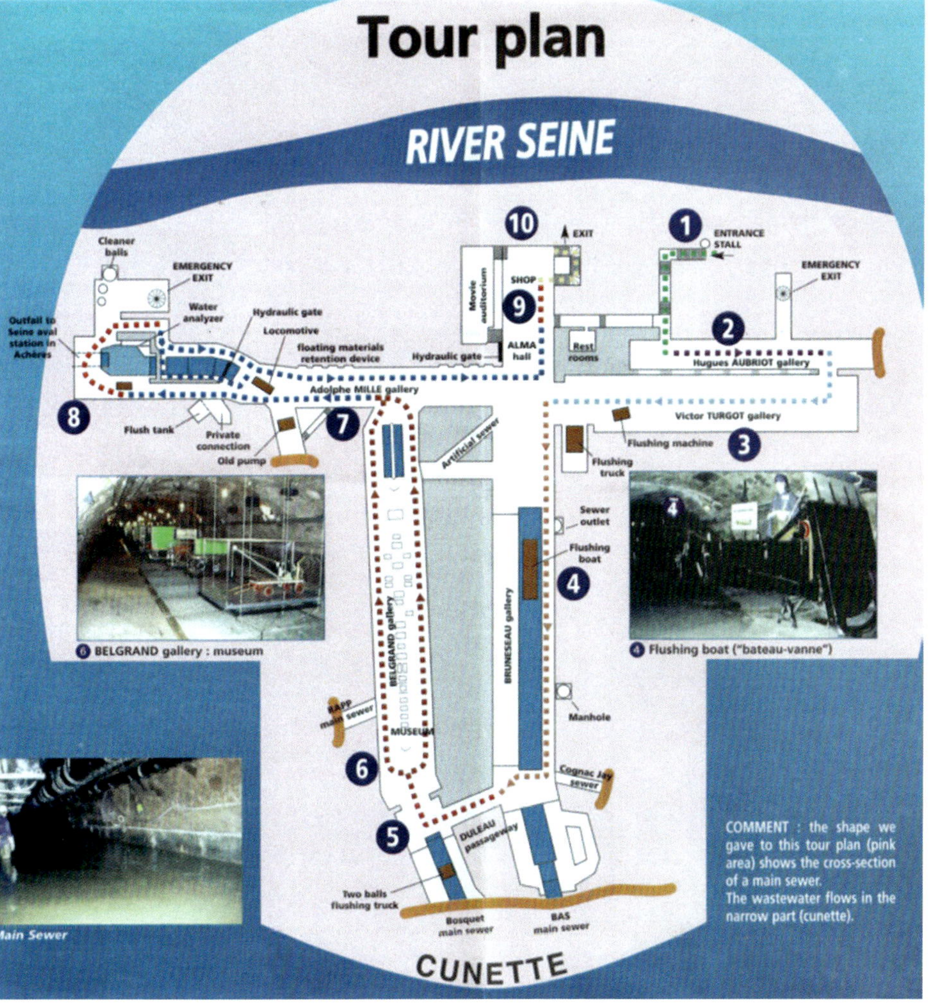


Before descending underground, take note of the city workers sweeping debris along the flooded gutters directly into the sewer system. (opposite page)

The Paris sewer system is unique in the world because not only does it manage sewage, it contains separate pipes for both drinking and non-drinking water, pneumatic tubes for transporting packages and mail, and telecommunication and traffic signal cables.

It is also one of the largest sewer systems in the world. The sewer collects 1,200,000 cubic meters of wastewater daily within its 1,312 miles of tunnels. That distance would take you from New York to Miami, all within the confines of Paris. It disposes of more than 15,000 cubic meters of solid waste, all of which is treated at one of the largest sewage treatment plants in Europe.

Despite its size, don't worry about getting lost. The tunnels run parallel to the streets above and the same elegant street signs tell you exactly where you are.

A variety of equipment is used to keep the sewage flowing, including flushing boats, dredgers, large wooden or steel balls, and much else. The tour explains the history and evolution of Paris's sewers in the context of the growth of the city. Some of the information was in English but most was in a technical French far beyond my comprehension. Still, I learned a bit.

In the early 1200s, Paris's streets were paved with open air drains. The first underground sewer in Paris dates to 1370 under rue Montmartre. Napoléon Bonaparte introduced covered sewers in the early 1800s. The engineer Eugene Belgrand designed the current system in 1850 as part of the overhaul of the city under Baron Haussmann's scheme. Since 1894, all wastewater was required by law to connect to the sewer system. Today, and perhaps despite appearances, the sewer treatment system, with its state-of-the-art treatment plant, is one of the most advanced in the world.

Displays describe in detail the work of the 800 égoutiers who maintain the sewer. Their pride in the work they do, the health hazards they face, their fight for labor rights, and how essential they are to the basic functioning of the city is emphasized throughout.

No museum is complete without a gift shop. Le Museé des Égouts is no exception. I recommend bringing home one of the darling stuffed rats. I'm sorry I didn't.

Like all underground arteries, the sewer provides a getaway and hideaway. True to Disney fiction, rats maximize these benefits, though they steered clear of me while I was there. More seriously, the French Resistance used it in WWII to evade the Germans. In Victor Hugo's *Les Misérables*, Jean Valjean escaped the barricades and carry the injured Marius to safety through the sewers.

In the book, Jean Valjean rhapsodized, ". . .[T]he great prodigality of Paris, her marvelous fête, her Beaujon folly, her orgy, her full-handed outpouring of gold, her pageant, her luxury, her magnificence, is her sewer."

In the end, the Ritz and les Égouts de Paris have more in common than one might think. Both have, in their own way, an abundance of gold, a pageantry, and a magnificence.

Public Service Announcement:

Fats, oils, grease and "flushable" wipes coalesce into fat-bergs, which are massive, costly, and dangerous blockages in sewer channels. Please take note that "flushable" wipes do not disintegrate and are a scourge to the proper functioning of any sewer.

One of the largest fat-bergs to date was discovered in September 2017 under Whitechapel in London. At 820 feet long, this rock-hard monster was longer than Tower Bridge and weighed over 140 tons or about as much as two Airbus A380 aircraft.

It took over two months of working seven days a week at a cost of more than £1 million to remove this fat-berg, using a combination of high-pressure water jets, jackhammers, and axes.

Next time you rinse something down your kitchen drain or flush your toilet, spare a thought for sewer systems and particularly for those who maintain them for our benefit.

A sewer clogged with a fat-berg in Cardiff

The same sewer after the fat-berg was removed

## Paris Gardens in the Spring

Gardens, gardens, everywhere. And parks. My goodness, the gardens and parks. Paris's gardens and parks are all the more welcome and spectacular in the spring because they banish the dreary darkness of the long winter.

Jardin des Tuileries, Jardin du Luxembourg, Jardin des Plantes, and Parc Monceau are public gardens in the middle of the city. You will find the Parc des Buttes-Chaumont on Paris's east end and, on the western outskirts of the city, the enormous Bois de Boulonge.

Winter in the Jardin des Tuileries

Spring in the Jardin des Tuileries

Late Spring in the Jardin de Tuileries

Jardin de Tuileries

Sunning around the Grand Basin Rond on a chilly early spring day in the Jardin des Tuileries

Sunday afternoon in the Parc Monceau

Musée Rodin Sculpture Garden

In the courtyard of the Musée Carnavalet

# Paris

March 15 to April 30, 2012

# 6 rue St. Lazare Redux

Paris was becoming a habit.

After two years away, I returned for a six-week stay in the same apartment as in 2010.

# April Fools' Day

Ancient Romans celebrated the springtime festival of Hilaria. As the name suggests, raucous merriment marked the transition from winter to spring. Some say this is the origin of April Fools' Day.

Some date the holiday to 1582, when the calendar switched from the Julian to the Gregorian, shifting the New Year from April 1st to January 1st. Some resisted the change. Others, in remote regions, didn't learn about it for months. People who continued to celebrate the New Year on April 1st were looked upon as fools. April 1st became a Fools' Day.

In France today, the holiday is known as Poisson d'avril (April fish). Fish became associated with April Fools' Day in French folklore as multitudes of fish spawn in the spring, making them easier to catch. Foolish April fish aren't savvy enough to avoid fishermen's lures.

April fish continue to multiple in various mediums. Greeting cards feature them. Chocolate shops mold them. French children stick paper cutouts of fish on peoples' backs. An elegantly dressed businessman walked by me on rue Rivoli with an orange fish taped to his back. I imagined him laughing when he realized he had been pranked, remembering his own childhood. I found a discarded paper fish, complete with tape, on the sidewalk. I picked it up as a souvenir of the day, feeling only a bit foolish. I bought myself a festive chocolate fish.

Any holiday with chocolate, no matter its origin, is well worth celebrating.

# A Day at the Races

One of the joys of being in Paris is experiencing it with other people whose interests and knowledge differ from mine. Jim, who was visiting with my sister Joan, wanted to go to the horse races.

Not knowing a thing about horse racing in or around Paris beyond the designer line of Longchamp, much internet research ensued. There are three tracks easily accessible from Paris. The Longchamp track was, regrettably, not running that weekend. The Auteuil track was running obstacle races, which was not of particular interest. We settled on Vincennes, which was running trotters.

Next step, getting ourselves there. We would take the red RER Line A from the Haussmann/St. Lazare station to the Joinville-le-Pont station stop and walk from there. [Note: Do NOT use the Vincennes stop.]

Maps in hand, off we trotted.

**Trouble out of the gate and confusion following the course**

Turnstiles and I don't always get along. On this particular day – I still don't know how I managed it – I found myself straddling the turnstile to get to the platform at Haussmann/St. Lazare.  One delinquent leg dangled on the wrong side of the turnstile bar. As I'm flaying about trying to extricate myself, the attendant takes notice. I start waving my Navigo pass in his direction, fearful that he might think I was trying to jump the turnstile.

Waving one hand, balancing precariously on one foot, and desperately trying to keep my shoulder bag from getting tangled around my knees, I was quite the slapstick act. Eventually, I unwound my contorted self and managed to get all of me on the right side of the turnstile. Still waving my Navigo pass at the bemused attendant, I stumbled onward.

Finally, out of the gate, now where do we turn? RER station stops are often shared with métro stations. Naturally, these tend to be larger stations with multiple levels and lots of activity.

There ensued much confusion as to where to find the right track. I asked half a dozen pre-occupied and otherwise uninterested passengers on the platform if this was the train going to Vincennes. They looked at me uncomprehendingly and returned to their pre-occupations. In their defense, my pronunciation of Vincennes was unintelligible to any French speaker.

A kind young man, taking pity on my ineptitude, came up to us and patiently deciphered my query. We were, indeed, in the wrong place. He pointed us upstairs. We were soon back on track to the races.

But the finish line was still a distance away.

The RER ride was uneventful, and we got off at the right station, praise the heavens. Fear, however, soon replaced my self-congratulatory mood. We were confronted with another set turnstiles to get out of the station. To exit, passengers had to swipe their ticket to show they had paid the proper fare.

Unbeknownst to me, the Joinville-le-Pont stop was outside Zone 1 of the métro system, which meant it was outside the limits of my dear and faithful Navigo pass. Joan and Jim, who had bought the proper individual tickets, sailed through the exit, no problem.

I swiped my pass, resulting in a nasty buzz and a damning red X. I tried again. A pixelated display next to the swipe area flashed the message that my pass was invalid. That machine was not going to be swayed by my innocent mistake.

I would have been happy to buy a proper ticket. The trouble was that the only ticket kiosks in sight were on the other side of the turnstile. An attendant helped Joan and Jim to the right kiosk to buy a ticket for me. The attendant then goes back to his business, leaving Joan and Jim to negotiate with the less than intuitive machine.

Marooned on the wrong side of our trip, not able to help Joan and Jim with their questions, I watch someone jump the turnstile. The attendant had left the window. Another woman comes along and is also stuck on the track side. At least I was not alone.

Joan comes over with another question. I don't have the answer. I begin to pace, if not quite panic. Then, I make a radical decision. I slip under the turnstile to the other side. I became the scofflaw I had so feared at the beginning of our journey. But at least we were all together and ready to go.


**Aaaaaaaannnnnnnnd, They're Off!**

Almost.

I had naively thought that, when we left the station, we would be able to find the racetrack without much difficulty. The problem was the Hippodrome is in the middle of the Bois de Vincennes, which covers 2,459 acres.

After getting turned around for several blocks close to the station, a French woman interrupted our huddle over the map to ask if she could help. Once she understood where we were headed, she made it her mission to get us there safe and sound. She took us by the hand, me literally, and went blocks and blocks out of her way until the Hippodrome was well within sight.

From the five percent of her enthusiastic conversation that I could understand as we hustled along, I gathered that she had a daughter and two granddaughters who lived in the United States. That was about as far as my Pimsleur French lesson recordings could get me. But lots of smiling and nodding on my part seemed to suffice. After profuse and sincere thanks, we headed toward the Hippodrome entrance, our own race finally run.

But, before we got inside, a gentleman saw us taking photos, realized we were visitors, and took it upon himself to escort us through the entrance. After a short conversation with the attendant, who seemed reluctant about whatever was being discussed, we were whisked into the VIP section, smack dab next to the winner's circle.

We had run our race and finished with a flourish thanks to the kindness of strangers.

PARIS
VINCENNES
LeTROT
9
5

# The Concorde Métro Station

Paris métro stations are destinations in their own right, with guidebooks devoted solely to their unique settings.

Not having read any guidebook in advance, the Concorde métro station's platform on Line 12 was a bit of a puzzlement. It featured pretty blue letters on individual tiles, seemingly placed at random. A word puzzle?

The more I used the station and the more my French vocabulary improved, I began to find words within this maze of letters. Quel cette, droit, publique, leurs and terminer emerged. Eventually, the answer was revealed.

SPOILER ALERT!

The tiles spell out the 1789 Revolution's Déclaration des Droits de l'Homme et du Citoyen. (Declaration of the Rights of Man* and of the Citizen), which codifies the Enlightenment's principles of liberty and equality.

These ideals were undercut a few years later during the Reign of Terror, which began in 1793. The Place de la Concorde played a particular grisly role when a guillotine was set up in its center. Over 2,600 people were beheaded as traitors to the revolution, including, most famously, Louis XVI and Marie Antoinette. Nearby residents complained about the stench of the blood.

Near the end of the Terror in February 1794, Robespierre, its prime architect, argued that violence was as necessary as virtue during a revolution:

> If the basis of popular government in peacetime is virtue, the basis of popular government during a revolution is both virtue and terror; virtue, without which terror is baneful; terror, without which virtue is powerless. Terror is nothing more than speedy, severe, and inflexible justice; it is thus an emanation of virtue.

A few months later, he would lose his own head.

* They did mean men. Women's right to vote in France was not fully granted until after WWII. L'Homme. Indeed.

Designed in 1755, the Place de la Concorde was originally named Place Louis XV, after the then current king. In 1789, it was renamed Place de la Révolution. Turbulent times being what they are, six years later it was renamed Place de la Concorde in a rather optimistic rebranding.

But concord was not to last. In 1814, when the Bourbon monarchy was restored, Louis XVIII, a brother of Louis XVI, changed its name back to Place Louis XV. In 1826, when Charles X, another brother of Louis XVI ascended the throne, he changed the name to Place Louis XVI. Four years later, the Bourbons were ousted again and the name changed back to the Place de la Concorde.

If the naming history of the Place de la Concorde is confusing, today's crazed traffic patterns in the multi-lane roundabout surrounding it are mind-boggling and can be as lethal as the guillotine.

I recommend avoiding all such dangers. Instead, take the métro and be inspired by some of the Enlightenment's loftiest principles.

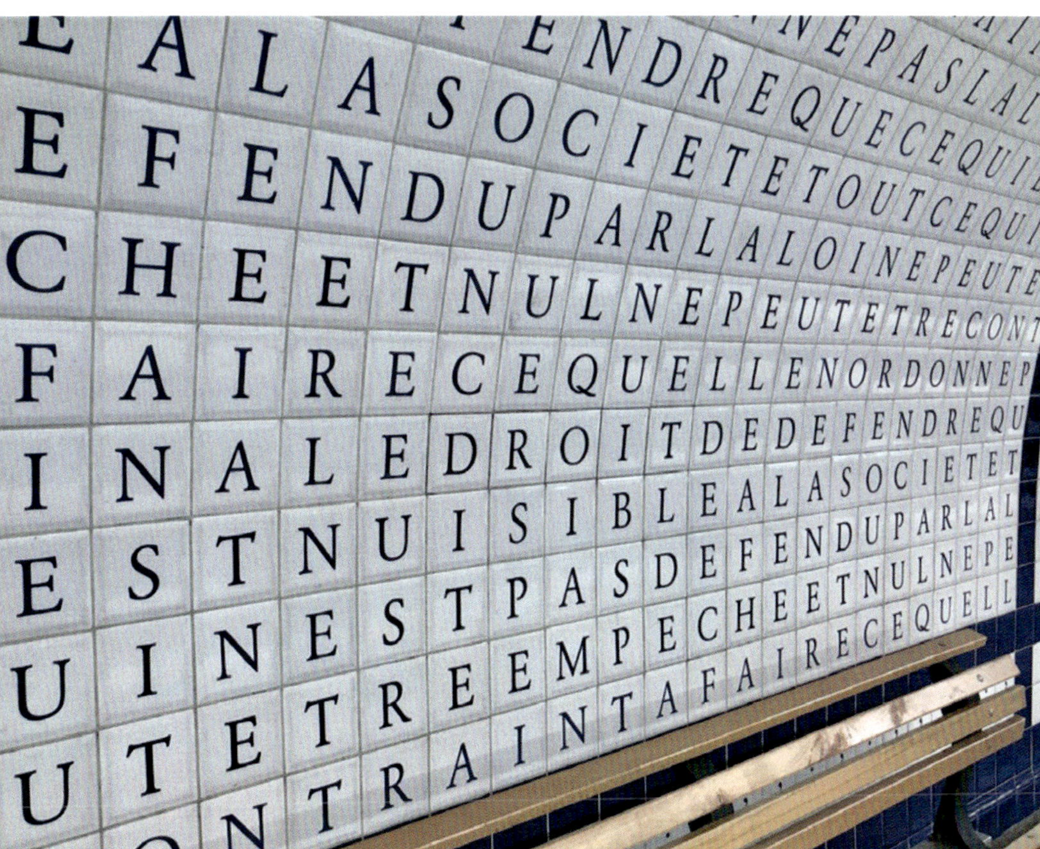

# Hidden Heroes of the Panthéon

The Panthéon in Paris dominates the Paris skyline along with the Eiffel Tower, Notre Dame Cathedral, and Sacré Cœur Basilica. It was designed in the mid-18th century to be a church and is modeled after the Panthéon in Rome. After several iterations, it was dedicated as a mausoleum in 1881, serving to memorialize France's National Heroes. Some have described the Panthéon as the republican equivalent of the Basilica of Saint-Denis, the necropolis of the French kings.

A hallowed, yet hollow place, it doesn't often make it into the top ten "must see" lists. The ground floor is cavernous and feels empty. A replica of Foucault's pendulum hangs from the center of the dome, alone in the vast rotunda. The paintings and sculptures dotting the walls are undoubtedly of interest and value to someone, but that someone is not me. The entrance to the austere crypt, containing the tombs or memorials, is nondescript.

A view of the Paris skyline from Notre Dame Cathedral with the Panthéon dome in the center

But I did my tourist duty. I gawped at the cold, massive marble interior. I stood mesmerized by Foucault's pendulum without understanding the underlying science*. I wandered down to the even colder crypt, paying my respects to a number of National Heroes, including Rousseau, Émile Zola, Victor Hugo, Voltaire, Jean Moulin, Toussaint Louverture, Louis Braille, Marie Skłodowska-Curie, and Josephine Baker. To be clear, not everyone who is panthéonised is buried in the Panthéon. Some are commemorated only by plaques or memorial structures.

It seemed an eclectic group of people, leading me to wonder how such an honor, known as panthéonisation, is determined. According to the Centre des Monuments Nationalaux's website, the chosen few deemed worthy of entering the Panthéon were first determined by the Constituent Assembly after the French Revolution. From 1804 until 1818, Napoléon Bonaparte, as Emperor, was the arbiter of the honor. Since then, parliaments or emperors have been the decision-makers until the Fifth Republic was established in 1958. Currently, the President of the Republic holds the key to the Panthéon's honors.

But enough of government sanctioned monuments. What interested me about the Panthéon, and the only thing that persuaded me to pay the small entrance fee, was a monumental, 19th century Wagner clock. It was time to explore the Panthéon for this hidden treasure.

What makes this clock such a treasure is a decidedly unsanctioned restoration. I first read about the clock's restoration in an article by Jon Lackmann in the January 20, 2012, edition of *Wired* magazine. Titled *The New French Hacker-Artist Underground*, it chronicles the activities of a clandestine group called UX, short for Urban eXperiment. Starting with a teenage boast in the early 1980s about about sneaking into the Panthéon, UX has developed over the decades into a disciplined organization.

Lackmann describes the organization of UX as:

> a cellular structure, with subgroups specializing in cartography, infiltration, tunneling, masonry, internal communications, archiving, restoration, and cultural programming. Its 100-odd members are free to change roles and are given access to all tools at the group's disposal. There is no manifesto, no charter, no bylaws—save that all members preserve its secrecy. Membership is by invitation only; when the group notices people already engaged in UX-like activities, it initiates a discussion about joining forces. While there is no membership fee, members contribute what they can to projects.

* The movement of Foucault's pendulum demonstrates the rotation of the earth on its axis. But appearances deceive. Although the pendulum appears to move in a circle with long, elliptical swings, it is actually the ground beneath the pendulum that is is moving. The motion is the rotation of earth on its axis. You can check it out in articles or online videos. It literally demonstrates the earth moving beneath your feet.

One subgroup of UX, called Untergunther* devotes itself to restoring invisible parts of French heritage. Lackmann interviewed the UX spokesman Lazar Kunstmann for his article. Explaining Kunstmann's views, Lackmann wrote, "French officials, he says, bother to protect and restore only the patrimony adored by millions—the Louvre, for example. Lesser-known sites are neglected, and if they happen to be out of public view—underground, say—they disintegrate totally, even when all that's needed is a hundred-dollar leak repair. UX tends the black sheep: the odd, the unloved, the forgotten artifacts of French civilization."

As of 2012, Untergunther had covertly restored more than fifteen historic artifacts. One, which necessarily became public, was the restoration of the Wagner clock between 2005 and 2006. The restoration team of eight members was overseen by Jean-Baptiste Viot, a Swiss trained master watchmaker and restorer. First, they established a workshop beneath the Panthéon's dome, carrying everything up the equivalent of fifteen stories, including armchairs, a library, lumber, cleaning fluids, drills, saws, and clock repair equipment. They even hauled up thick red curtains to help insulate the cold space, since, as Voit said, "a clockmaker can't do anything with mittens on."

In assessing the clocks condition, they discovered that someone had sabotaged the clock's escape wheel. With Viot's training, the team cleaned every surface of the clock's rusted mechanism. They repaired the cabinet, pulleys, and cables. The escape wheel had to be wholly reconstructed. They scavenged machinery for the clock's mechanism from different parts of the building. In all, they spent over €4,000 of their own money to restore the Wagner clock.

With the clock finally restored to working order, someone would need to wind it regularly to keep it ticking. Untergunther broke their anonymity and told the director of the museum about the restoration. According to one source, the director did not even know the Pantheon had a clock but was enthused about the restoration and publicly praised Untergunther. Regrettably, the Centre des Monuments Nationaux did not share his enthusiasm, being embarrassed by the gross lack of security.

The director was forced into early retirement. His deputy, who had allegedly been angling for the directorship, took over. The new director perversely hired a clockmaker to re-sabotage the clock. Instead, the clockmaker merely disengaged the escape wheel, which UX retrieved, holding it for safekeeping in the event a future director would welcome the return of the Wagner clock's chime. In the meantime, the clock face is permanently set at 10:51. Whether a.m. or p.m. is unknown.

---

* Lazar Kunstmann says the name was inspired by Unter and Gunther, the names of imaginary guard-dogs in the Arènes de Chaillot's security system.

The French government sued UX twice and lost twice. As Lackmann concluded, "There is no law in France, it turns out, against the improvement of clocks."

But, back to my search for the Wagner clock in its quiet, still state. I wasn't sure of the exact location of the clock, but I knew I needed to make my way back to the rotunda from the crypt. Following some signs with a little white man running on a green background saying "sortie," which means exit, I found myself at a little green gate. The gate was unlocked so I opened it and climbed the narrow stairs that led to a large wooden door.

Peeking through a gap in the door, I was pleased to see the rotunda. Gently pushing the door open, I slipped out – right into the back of the security guard's desk. With a stern look, he began to make calls on his walkie talkie.

Ummm. My bad. I guess the little white man on the sortie sign was for emergencies only. I smiled meekly like the dumb tourist I was, and he let me go on my way.

I never did find the clock but, in true UX fashion, I like to think that I uncovered my own security breach. I also like to think that the members of Untergunther are, in their own unique, if clandestine way, as much national heroes as the politicians, writers, scientists and activists who have been panthéonised. The Wagner clock is their memorial.

I later learned that the Wagner clock is above the doorway
to Rondelet's scale model of the Panthéon.

## Graffiti by the Numbers

On a random street corner, someone spray-painted a graphic of the Fibonacci spiral.

The Fibonacci spiral is the visual representation of the Fibonacci sequence 1, 1, 2, 3, 5, 8, 13, 21, 34, 55 . . ., where each number is the sum of the two preceding numbers.

In the form of an equation, it is $F(n) = F(n-1) + F(n-2)$ for $n > 0$.

The spiral starts in two 1x1 squares, then circles into a 2x2 square, followed by a 3x3 square, a 5x5 square, ad infinitum, matching the sequence. It is found in nature in everything from seashells to tree branches to flower petals and even to the side view of a human fist.

I love Paris.

# Paris

May 31 to June 30, 2018

# 38 rue de Chateâudon, 9th arr.
## Métro: Trinitè-D'Estienne d'Orves (Line 12)

After a six-year hiatus, I was able to return to Paris. My apartment this year was a mix of Hausmann architecture, IKEA decor, an exquisite courtyard garden, capped with a dose of literary history, and more than a bit of confusion.

A delayed flight meant I couldn't check-in on time. After staying overnight in a hotel, the owner hurriedly met me the next morning on his way to work. Despite this, he carefully explained the front door lock. The lock was not your normal: (1) insert the key; (2) turn the key; and (3) opened the door lock. The owner showed me some combination of lifting the door handle, inserting the key, rotating it  one way for a half rotation, then the opposite way for a full rotation, while pulling down the handle. Or something like that. He showed me twice and had me open it by myself.

That success was clearly beginner's luck, as I discovered the first time I went out. My attempt to open the door when I returned introduced me to the lock gremlins. They were cunning little fellows. As soon as they had me on my own, they went to work. They changed up the sequence of the lock's function. Every single day. Sometimes it was this way, then it was that. But, sometimes it was that way, then this. Sometimes the handle needed to be moved up. Sometimes down.

Clever but not nasty gremlins. They never actually locked me out. They just wanted their little fun while I stood outside sweating with frustration and worry. After a while, my incompetence must have been less entertaining and opening the lock became easier.

Once inside, the apartment was as expected. Simple, clean and good enough. IKEA through and through. The space was exceptionally large for a studio. The tiny kitchen even had its own door, a couple of electric burners, a toaster oven, and a clothes washer.

What the apartment didn't have was toilet paper. Fortunately, a nearby Franprix grocery was open. A confusing plethora of cleaning products were scattered among the cupboards. Long consultations with my French dictionary and translation app kept me from using liquid bath scrub on the dishes.

At night, when the floor length windows were secured with a thick metal shade, the apartment became a tomb. This had all the benefits of quiet and darkness, certainly conducive to a good night's rest. Regrettably, it also had the disadvantage of suffocation, which matters less to occupants of actual tombs than to it did to me. My second purchase was a fan, which doubled as a clothes dryer.

Which brings us to the matter of the clothes washer. The washer had only three buttons and one dial, simple French labeling, and pictographs. But damned if I could figure it out. On the first go-round, it filled with water, spun the clothes clean and rinsed them. After the rinse cycle, however, it refused to spin them dry. The number of combinations of button pushing and dial settings was surprisingly endless. Ultimately, I settled on hand-wringing the clothes, and having them drip dry on the vinyl-tiled floor. Thank you, IKEA.

My confusion slowly gave way to a comfortable stay.

## The Neighborhood

All three of my first apartments were in the 9th arrondissement, north of the Seine and away from the main tourist attractions.

Rue des Martyrs, a traditional shopping street, was close by. It was lined with local shops specializing in cheeses, breads, fish, meats, fruits, or wine. A housewares/hardware store and a church were only a couple of blocks away. The neighborhood had everything necessary to meet spiritual, practical, and edible needs.

A First Communion class on the steps of Notre Dame de Lorette Church. The church itself felt almost derelict inside, but it was a sweetly calm refuge too. I was glad to see it had an active congregation.

The housewares/hardware store on rue des Martyrs.
This supplied the clothes-drying rack for the rue Saint Lazare apartment
in 2012 and the fan for the rue de Châteaudon apartment in 2018.

PATISSERIE
BOULANGERIE
VIENNOISERIE

VIENNOIS
BOULANGERIE
MAISON LANDEMAINE
ARTISAN BOULANGER
RUE MANUEL

Many local shops along rue des Martyrs were giving way to international chain stores. The little boulangerie was one of the local shops that had closed, though its fate was uncertain when this photo was taken in 2023.

A boulangerie in 2007 (opposite page top), 2012 (opposite page bottom), and 2023 (above)

## Shakespeare and Company

I confess to a snobbery that kept me from seeking out the Shakespeare and Company bookstore on previous trips. After all, it is not THE Shakespeare and Company established in 1919 by Sylvia Beach who published James Joyce's *Ulysses* in 1922. Phffft! That bookshop closed in December 1941 during the German Occupation and never re-opened.

I must now humbly admit the current Shakespeare and Company has a virtue and deserved prestige of its own.

George Whitman opened the current shop in 1951 under the name Le Mistral. The name was changed to Shakespeare and Company in 1964 with Sylvia Beach's blessing. Today, George's daughter, Sylvia Whitman, owns and manages the store where she has kept up the tradition of the store's "tumbleweeds." The tumbleweeds are aspiring writers and artists who are allowed to bed down in the store's nooks and aisles in exchange for helping out in the bookstore. The shop's motto, "Be Not Inhospitable to Strangers Lest They Be Angels in Disguise," is literally lived out amongst its shelves.

Thank goodness I finally sought it out. It is a delightful and veritable warren of jammed bookshelves and narrow aisles. I left with the perfect book for my sojourn here, *Images and Shadows: Part of a Life*, a memoir by Iris Origo. And a reminder that snobbery never pays.

37 Rue de la Bûcherie

Edited by
KRISTA HALVERSON
SHAKESPEARE AND COMPANY
A History of
the Rag
& Bone Shop
of the Heart
INDEPENDENT BOOKSTORE
KILOMETER ZERO PARIS

# Maps and Me

I like maps.

I have a box of maps at home. I have a copy of the 10th Comprehensive Edition of the Times Atlas of the World, weighing over twelve pounds. I have several map apps on my smartphone. I keep AAA folding maps in my glove compartment and I carry compact paper maps of city streets and public transportation when I travel.

I enjoy wandering the streets of Paris and have often enjoyed being lost there. But, sometimes, I would like to efficiently navigate my way home after a long day with blistered feet.

Alas. In these instances, maps fail me.  For all my love of maps, I suffer from directional dyslexia. It's one thing to trace out a journey with a flat map on one's dining room table. It is quite another to be on a crowded sidewalk, trying to figure out where one is standing. With street names changing at random intersections and corners with six different ways to turn, with paper maps that can be twisted in any direction, and phone maps that twirl about as one moves, without intuitively knowing north from south or being able to track the sun's path, I'm left helpless.

Several times on this trip I was caught out in my personal Bermuda Triangle with l'Opéra Garnier at its center. I tried to maneuver the streets from the Tuileries to my apartment (south to north) only to arrive home exhausted, walking ten times further than necessary.

The other day, I was entering the Concorde métro stop as people were rushing up the stairs, yelling at those going down to turn around. Flames, smoke, and explosive noises had erupted at the back of the Line 12 train I was to take. With the November 2015 terror attacks still raw in peoples' memories, everyone's first thought was that a bomb exploded. Fortunately, this concern was quickly dispelled. What was probably an electrical short did, however, shut down the train and station.

After investigating the underground situation, I decided to walk back to the apartment. Theoretically, the shortest way was straight through my personal Bermuda Triangle. You can guess what happened next.

In my feeble defense, the area covers three arrondissements, meaning I had to consult three different page spreads of my detailed Paris Circulation booklet. My phone map apps left me dizzy with their spinning as I turned about. Yes, I managed to get turned around and lost within a few blocks. Finally, a métro stop appeared like a lifeboat in the fog.

One map I have been able to read like a pro is the métro map. You don't have to know streets. Just the numbers and corresponding colors of métro lines, and the end stop of the direction you want to go.

The métro stop was on a line I hadn't taken before, but it got me back to Line 12, which was running again. So down I went and, voilà! I soon emerged at the Trinité stop with a clear shot and short walk home to my apartment.

Today, I'm going to try a different tack and traverse the Triangle in the opposite direction, north to south, leaving from my apartment. In the perverse universe of my mind and maps, maybe that will make more sense.

If not and I am never heard from again, you'll know that I am wandering somewhere in the middle of my personal Parisian Bermuda Triangle. Forever lost. Just me and my maps.

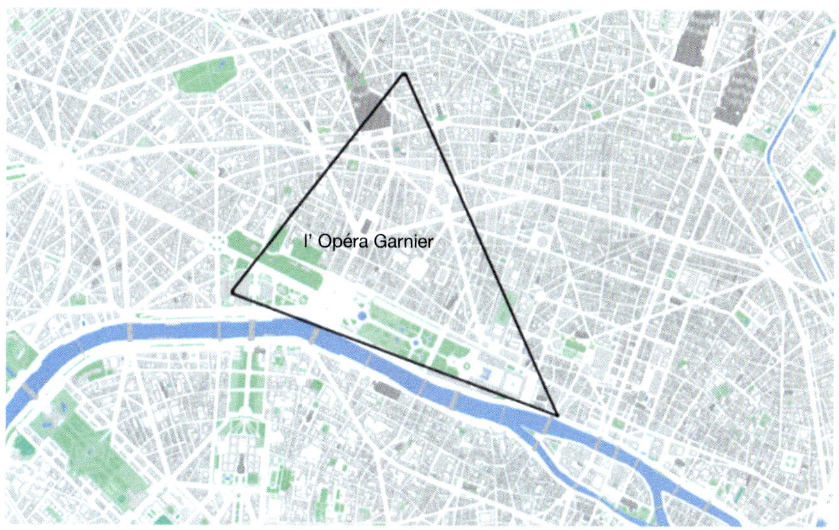

## Rue Saint Jacques

One of my self-taught language programs repeated and repeated and repeated (and repeated) the question, "Ou est la rue Saint Jacques?" ("Where is Saint Jacques Street?")

I can finally and definitively answer, "La rue Saint Jacques est ici." ("Saint Jacques Street is here.")

At last!

# The Pigeon, the Goose, and the Swan

The title of a children's book? A philosophical treatise on identity?

A pigeon

A goose

A swan

Or just another day in the Tuileries Gardens?

# Versailles

Some friends who had been to Versailles dismissed it by saying, "It is big. It is crowded. It has a lot of gold." I chafed at this description. Surely, not just that.

A three-volume memoir by duc de Saint-Simon recorded in wry, gossipy detail the daily life of Louis XIV's and Louis XV's courts in Versailles. It was a place full of intrigue and wildly extravagant entertainments. Even the ennui of courtiers with nothing to do all day was fraught with tension. Surely, the site retained some vestiges of this history.

So, I went to Versailles.

It was big. It was crowded. It had a lot of gold.

Far right, a line of tourists wait to get tickets, with the entrance in the center behind the golden gate.

While standing in the opulent Hall of Mirrors, I tried to conjure up the emotions of the diplomats when they signed the Treaty of Versailles in 1919, which ended the First World War and carved the globe into winners and losers. It was overwhelming. By which I mean the crowds were overwhelming. We had to mostly shuffle along so the mass of tourists behind us could shuffle along too.

The Hall of Mirrors

We toured the palace in the conveyor-belt line of fellow underwhelmed onlookers. We had a bite to eat at the Grand Café d'Orléans, with its modern, cafeteria-style decor. We walked back to the station and went home.

Alone, I went to Versailles again, determined to find at least a glimmer of the duc de Saint-Simon's world. And, still …

It was big. It was crowded. It had a lot of gold.

It was a drizzly weekday and the fountains were turned off. My strategy was to avoid the crowds around the main palace and wander through the grounds to Le Petit Trianon, a château built in the mid-1760s. Louis XV commissioned it for use by his mistress Madame du Barry. Later it was used by Marie Antoinette to escape the stultifying atmosphere of the court. Her hermitage, where she notoriously played peasant while Parisians starved, is next door.

Angelina's, which has its flagship restaurant on the rue Rivoli, has a small outdoor café next to the Petit Trianon. It is renown for its incredibly thick, incredibly rich, hot chocolate, which is particularly appropriate for its location near the Petit Trianon. Madame du Barry was fond of the drink, not least for its supposed aphrodisiac qualities. King Louis XV apparently felt the same as he had his own recipe.

---

Louis XV's Hot Chocolate Recipe

Place an equal number of bars of chocolate and cups of water in a cafetière and boil on a low heat for a short while; when you are ready to serve, add one egg yolk for four cups and stir over a low heat without allowing to boil. It is better if prepared a day in advance. Those who drink it every day should leave a small amount as flavouring for those who prepare it the next day. Instead of an egg yolk one can add a beaten egg white after having removed the top layer of froth. Mix in a small amount of chocolate from the cafetière then add to the cafetière and finish as with the egg yolk.

Source: *Dinners of the Court or the Art of working with all sorts of foods for serving the best tables following the four seasons*, by Menon, 1755 (BnF, V.26995, volume IV, p.331)

---

The walk from the entrance had been long and hot, and I was ready for a sit-down. Sadly, hot chocolate, despite its historic resonance, was not appealing in the least. I compromised on a chocolate eclair and fresh orange juice. I could not prod my imagination back to the 17th or 18th centuries.

Sipping my orange juice and poking at my eclair, I looked at the short security line for entry into the Petit Trianon. I just didn't care about seeing another opulent, tourist-ladened building. I paid my bill.

At the checkout, the young Frenchman immediately knew I was from the United States. He wanted to practice his English and was enamored of the American West. When he asked where I was from, I told him New Mexico, which was unknown to him and understandably confusing. So, I explained it was between Texas and California. His face lit up when he heard Texas and began to tell me how much he had wanted to be a cowboy when he was growing up.

I walked back to the main palace, off the grounds, and on to the train back to Paris.

I don't know what to say about Versailles. Go if you must. Let me know if you find the ghost of duc de Saint-Simon. But don't be surprised if Texas cowboys feel more real than the ghost of duc de Saint-Simon.

Tourist tip: If you go on a weekday when the gardens are free, expect to encounter an unconscionable number of children. So many, many tiny people. So very, very, very much noise from so many, many, many, many little mouths. God bless schoolteachers.

Versailles's grounds hold the title of the World's Largest Royal Domain as measured by total area, covering 2,014 acres. Wear your hiking boots.

# Life's Absurdity

As you may have noticed, I am prone to pedantic pretensions. Literary cafés play perfectly into that weakness.

I was sitting upstairs in Café de Flore, the former haunt of Jean-Paul Sartre and other writers and philosophers. Sipping my café crème, I was trying to think profound thoughts, bordering on a melancholic mood.

Sartre is not jolly a companion. In 1956, he published his definitive work, *On Being and Nothingness: An Essay on Phenomenological Ontology*. Oy. My pretensions do not extend to reading my way through that 900-plus pages of dense language. My brain fogs over just reading summaries.

Sartre is best known for his articulation of Existentialism as a philosophical school. I'll let Wikipedia summarize:

> a central proposition of existentialism is that existence precedes essence, which is to say that individuals shape themselves by existing and cannot be perceived through preconceived and a priori categories, an "essence". The actual life of the individual is what constitutes what could be called their "true essence" instead of an arbitrarily attributed essence others use to define them. Human beings, through their own consciousness, create their own values and determine a meaning to their life. This view is in contradiction to Aristotle and Aquinas, who taught that essence precedes individual existence.

Got that? Me either.

Sartre had a friend, Albert Camus, who also frequented Café de Flore until he and Sartre fell out.

Camus was a novelist, essayist, journalist, and playwright. I have read most of Camus's work and found solace in his understanding of life's value. Being one of those people tormented with questions like: What is the point of existing? What does it all mean? When life becomes unbearable, why not choose death over life? For me, Camus had an answer.

Rejecting Existentialism, Camus adopts the Paradox of the Absurd, most clearly described in his 1942 essay Le Mythe de Sisyphe. As the myth tells, Sisyphus offended the gods and was condemned to repeatedly and forever roll a boulder up a hill in the Underworld. Camus turns this myth on its head and finds a sort of optimism in Sisyphus's fate.

Café de Flore
CAFE DE FLORE

Camus notes that, after Sisyphus rolls the boulder up the hill, he turns and walks back down. Camus focuses on Sisyphus's return. Despite the absurdity of his task, Sisyphus embraces his fate every time he turns to walk back down the hill. Camus concludes, "The struggle itself towards the heights is enough to fill man's heart. One must imagine Sisyphus happy."

I'm distracted from these thoughts by a well-dressed Parisienne. She is wearing shockingly red nail polish. My mind drifts to daydreaming about shades of red and painting my nails.

Life goes absurdly on. Should I try a Ruby Red or Scarlet Starlet?

  The view from my upstairs table at Café de Flore

## Parisian Cafés

From my notebook as read in Café de Flore:

> For the point [of cafés] is not profit or usefulness, but only pleasure and well-being, intelligence, and discussion.
>
> ~ Patrick Kéchichian in *Le Monde*

> The world is a comedy for those who think and a tragedy for those who feel.
>
> ~ Horace Walpole

Of the many cultural experiences Paris offers, my hands-down favorite is cafés. For the price of an expensive cup of coffee you can sit forever and a day, solitary but not lonely, contemplating the cosmos and watching human dramas unfold.

My favorite cafés are the more formal, with waiters wearing a uniform of black pants, white shirt, black vest, and a long white apron. Serving coffee has a ritual element. The coffee and crème are served separately, each in its own warmed pitcher with sugar cubes wrapped in paper and a little cookie on the side of the saucer. One can get very Zen in a Japanese tea ceremony kind of way, choosing the order and portions of pouring coffee and crème. More practically, in my bag lady kind of way, I usually drop the sugar cubes and cookie in my purse. Not very zen but it makes for a nice treat later in the day.

A typical breakfast setting at Le Select

Traditional cafés are an odd combination of formality and relaxation. The waiters exude such efficient competence with an air of superiority.  It can be intimidating. But, if you become a regular customer and know the proper etiquette, the waiters can become quite charming. One even gave me a wink as he brought a second small, complimentary pitcher of coffee to the table.

One of my favorite moments this trip was in the Café de Flore watching a little drama played out by three waiters. They were having an animated discussion, looking down a long line of unoccupied chairs. After much gesturing and shaking of heads, one walked over to a chair in the middle of the row and moved it not more than inch toward its table. He returned to the other two who nodded approvingly as they gauged the now straight line. I think they were half-joking with one another but only half-joking. I was glad to be in on the joke, intentionally or not.

Five thousand, one hundred and forty-one miles is no distance at all to travel for the pleasure of sitting in a Parisian café.

Note to US coffee drinkers: refills are not part of Parisian café culture. If you want more than one cup, you must place another order.

## Transitions

It was time to go home. Until the last moment, I was still seeking cafés. It wasn't the same, but, at least my name was spelled en français.

A vente latte from Starbucks at Aéroport de Paris Charles-de-Gaulle

# PART II

## La Grande Expédition
## Santa Fe to Paris

---

December 22, 2019

to

January 16, 2020

Since my trip in 2018, I wondered what it would be like to travel from Santa Fe to Paris without taking an airplane. The journey as an adventure, not just an expedient. A Grand Expedition.

**Itinerary for La Grande Expédition**
**December 2019 to May 2020**

**Santa Fe to Brooklyn**

| | |
|---|---|
| 12/22 | Drive from Santa Fe to Denver |
| 12/22 to 12/26 | Stay with family in Denver |
| 12/26 | RTD Light rail Train E to Denver Union Station<br>Overnight on Amtrak to Naperville train station |
| 12/27 to 1/1 | Stay with family in Naperville |
| 1/1 | Drive to Naperville train station<br>Metra Train to Chicago Union Station<br>Overnight on Amtrak to New York Penn Station |
| 1/2 to 1/3 | Taxi to Brooklyn<br>Overnight at Brooklyn Motor Inn |

**Brooklyn to London**

| | |
|---|---|
| 1/3 to 1/10 | Walk to Brooklyn Pier<br>Sail QM2 to Southampton Pier |
| 1/10 | Taxi to Southampton Coach Station<br>National Express bus to London Victoria Coach Station<br>Victoria Tube Line to St. Pancras/King's Cross Station<br>Walk to Crestfield Hotel |
| 1/10 to 1/16 | Stay at Crestfield Hotel |

**London to Paris**

| | |
|---|---|
| 1/16 | Walk to St. Pancras Station<br>Eurostar to Gare du Nord<br>Metro Line 4 to 25 blvd de Sébastopol |
| 1/16 to 4/17 | Stay at 25 blvd de Sébastopol |

**Paris to Santa Fe**

| | |
|---|---|
| 4/17 | Metro Line 4 to Gare due Nord<br>Eurostar to St. Pancras<br>Victoria Tube Line to Victoria Coach Station<br>Bus to Southampton Coach Station Harbor<br>Taxi to Mayview Guest House |
| 4/17 to 4/18 | Overnight at Mayview Guest House |
| 4/18 to 4/25 | Taxi to Southampton Pier<br>Sail QM2 to Brooklyn Pier |
| 4/25 to 4/26 | Taxi to New Yorker Hotel<br>Overnight at New Yorker Hotel |
| 4/26 | Walk to Penn Station<br>Overnight on Amtrak to Chicago Union Station |
| 4/27 | Change trains at Chicago Union Station |
| 4/27 | Overnight on Amtrak to Denver Union Station |
| 4/28 | RTD Light Rail Train E to Oak Station |
| 4/28 to May 3 | Stay with family in Denver |
| 5/3 | Drive to Santa Fe |

This was the plan. But, as we know, "The best laid plans of mice and men do often go astray." (*To A Mouse*, Robert Burns) The second half of this itinerary was waylaid by world events. But, more of that later.

# Santa Fe to Brooklyn

# Santa Fe to Denver

I-25 north between Las Vegas and Raton, New Mexico

# Denver to Naperville

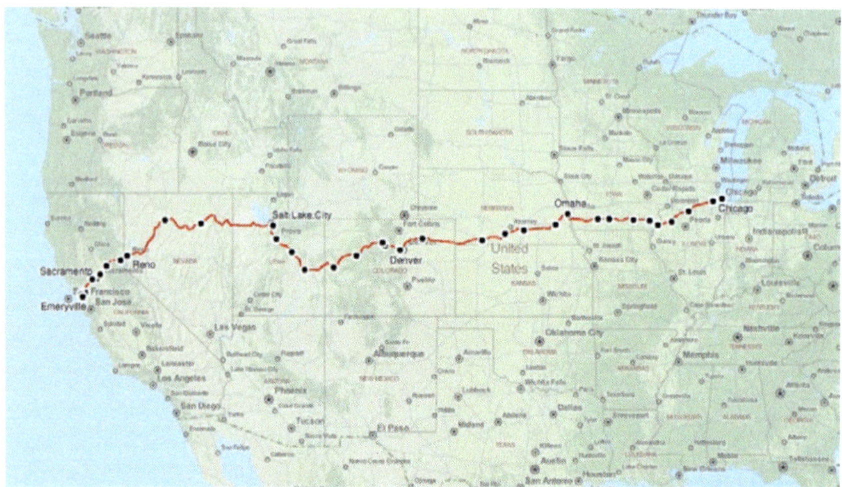

California Zephyr route map

My sleeper roomette on the California Zephyr

# Naperville to Brooklyn

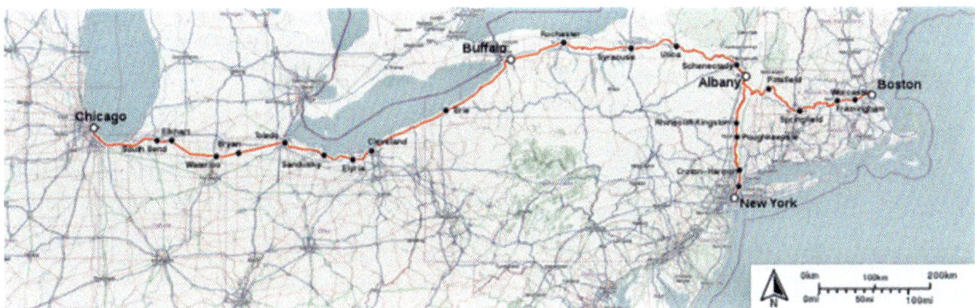

Lake Shore Limited route map

Chicago Union Station

View of Manhattan skyline from the QM2

View from the gangway while boarding (opposite page)

# The North Atlantic

## At Sea

The Stars Above the Sea

*Far, far away one mystery greets*
*Another vast and high,*
*The infinite of waters meets*
*The infinite of sky.*

Amos Russel Wells (1862 - 1933)

# The Queen Mary 2

A winter North Atlantic cruise? Sign me up. None of these lay-back-on-the-sun-deck-with-a-piña-coloda Caribbean cruises. Uh uh. Give me cold, harsh winds, long, dark nights, and nothing but ocean for days and days.

Several cruise lines make Transatlantic voyages, but Cunard's QM2 is the only purpose-built ocean liner in service. I booked months in advance to snag one of the few single staterooms, trying to keep to some sort of budget. But Poseidon, or a Cunard reservations clerk in some cubicle, decided my love of the ocean should be fully indulged and I was unexpectedly upgraded from my tiny interior single room to a luxurious balcony suite. Sweet, indeed.

I've seen enough old movies to have an outdated, naïvely romantic notion about Transatlantic ships and who I would meet onboard. My modern reality was that most people only wanted to compare the quality of the food service on different cruises they'd taken. I started to carry a book as an excuse to avoid people.

One exception was during Afternoon Tea in The Queens Room. All of the tables were set for four and, being solo, I was seated with a Bulgarian couple, who spoke English. They were classical musicians, who, years ago, overstayed their visas when traveling to Northern Ireland. Eventually, they settled in a tiny village near the border with the Republic of Ireland. They had remarkable stories of humorous misunderstandings caused by the differences in Bulgarian and Irish customs and of their eventual integration into this tight knit Irish community. I asked whether Brexit would affect their immigration status. They were uncertain but optimistic. I didn't see them again and can only hope their optimism was well placed.

Mostly, though, I was content to lean over my balcony railing, sipping the New Mexico Gruet sparkling wine given to me as a bon voyage gift, and watch the endless ocean for endless hours. I raised a glass to toast Poseidon and the Cunard reservations clerk who made this an extraordinary venture.

The iconic Cunard smokestack (opposite page)

## Stormy Weather

The Atlantic brewed up a winter storm shortly after we passed north of Canada. Even the ship's state-of-the-art stabilizers couldn't calm the heaving to and fro. Though I spent the night doing my own heaving into the toilet, the waves were magnificent.

## A Celestial Companion

Every now and then while traveling alone, I miss having a companion. This trip I had an unusual buddy, Orion.

The constellation Orion

Orion was shining brightly outside the front door the night before I left Santa Fe. It was comfortingly glowing outside the window of my sleeper car in the middle of Nebraska.

Although the skies were too cloudy to see, I knew it was amongst the stars over the North Atlantic. It would greet me in London as the days quickly turned to early nights. It would welcome me in Paris through my apartment window. It was a constant in the midst of constant movement.

The stars in Orion range from about 250 to over 1,300 light years away from Earth but, one night aboard the QM2, I got up close and personal to one. The Chart Room bar featured a menu of celestially-themed drinks. I ordered a drink called Bellatrix.

Bellatrix is one of the four navigational stars in Orion. The name in Arabic is Al Najīd, which loosely translated, means Conqueror.

The menu was effusive:

> From the star of Bellatrix reports
> this effervescent fusion that promotes
> the traits of any warrior, delicately fusing
> the wise sweet notes of Pisco with
> the regal uniformity and respect of Sake.

No idea what any of that means. But, hey, a reliable buddy, a conquering woman, navigational assistance. I think I'll order another round.

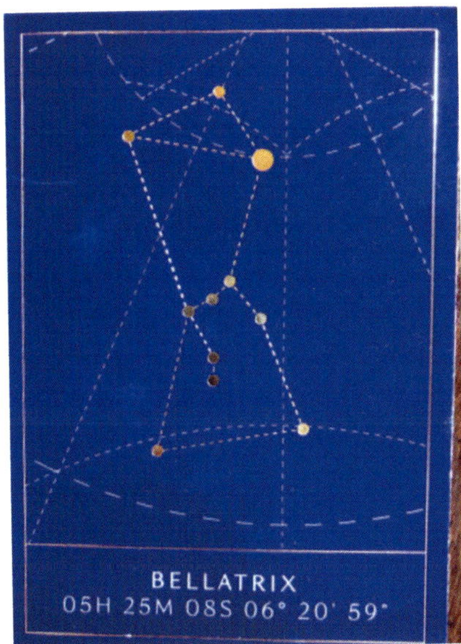


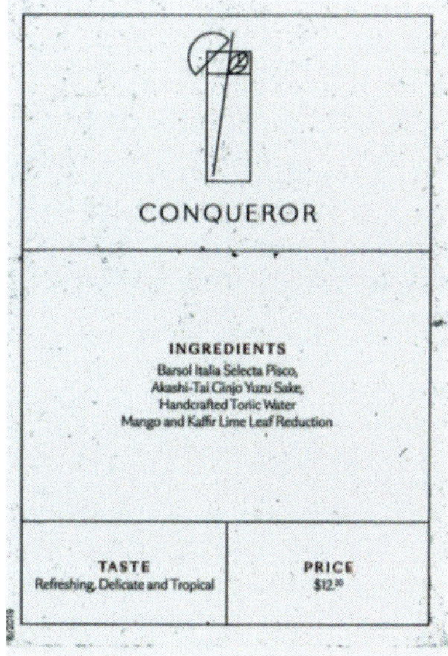


The drink card on the table

## Time Zones

Traveling east on the QM2 from Brooklyn to Southampton, we "lost" about an hour a day.

I began to wonder about time zones and took myself up to the library on Deck 8. There I found the oversized Times Comprehensive Atlas of the World, fittingly dedicated to Her Majesty, The Queen.

Theoretically, there are twenty-four time zones, one for each hour of the day. But, according to the Internet Assigned Numbers Authority's time zone database, there are over 200 time zones in the world today. In reality, time zones are complex, a complexity I was curious to understand.

I worked out the time for each day of the voyage:

January 4th        GMT -5.00 (Eastern Standard Time)
January 5th        GMT -4.00 (Puerto Rico and US Virgin Islands Time)
January 5-6th      GMT -3.30 (Newfoundland Standard Time)
January 6th        GMT -3.00 (Brazil Eastern Time)
January 7th        GMT -2.00
January 8th        GMT -1.00 (Central African Time)
January 9th        GMT  0.00 (Greenwich Mean Time)

Hmm. GMT -2.00 doesn't have a landmass assigned to it. Odd. And Newfoundland has its own time zone on the half hour? Whaaaaat?

Down the rabbit hole I went.

Newfoundland is not alone in setting its time to fractions of an hour. Many countries in Southern Asia commonly use half hour time zones. India, which holds about a fifth of the world's population, is in GMT +5:30. Who knew? (Well, billions of people know, but I didn't.) Nepal is GMT +5.75.

In addition to politics, the muddled business of time zones depends on evolving trade and communication needs. This is evidenced by the fact that the Interstate Commerce Commission has authority over time zone boundaries in the US. The goal of imposing uniformity on a multitude of inconsistent factors inevitably leads to an imperfect, sometimes chaotic, definition of time in any given locale.

Time zones also shift with political winds. In the last decade, North Korea switched its time zone twice. It had been in the same time zone as Japan. Then, it changed to China's time zone. Then, it changed back to Japan's. Sometimes, it's hard to keep up with the times.

The muddled business of times zones depends on evolving trade and communication needs (the Interstate Commerce Commission has authority over time zone boundaries in the US), assertions of national identity and the development of new technologies. Regulating time is fraught with factions of interest. Its goal of imposing uniformity on inherent differences, contingent on a multiplicity of factors, is inevitably imperfect, which is to say . . .

Oh dear. My mind was drifting dangerously off course. What was it I was looking for? Umm . . . oh, yes. Time zones crossing the Atlantic and what's up with GMT -2.0?

Eventually, I found an answer. The land masses within GMT -2.0 are two sets of archipelagos governed by Brazil and some small islands that are part of the British Overseas Territories. The Brazilian archipelago of Fernando de Noronha has a population of just over 3,100. None of the other islands have permanent residents. About thirty people from the British Antarctic Survey occasionally live on South Georgia and some other islands have research stations.

Traveling through the least populated time zone on Earth, being one of 0.0000001 percent of the world's population who occupied that time zone for the better part of one day, has to count among the most unique experiences of my life. An admittedly abstract, arbitrarily defined experience, but one that I nevertheless treasure.

The South Georgia and South Sandwich Islands as indicated by the black oval; the Brazilian archipelago of Fernando de Noronha is indicated by the red oval

Fun Fact 1:
It is possible to be in three different time zones while standing in one place – the spot where Norway, Finland and Russia share a border.

Fun Fact 2:
Until 1911, the French placed the prime meridian in Paris, which put Paris Mean Time at GMT -0.9.21 Oh, those French.

Map of Standard Time Zones

# London Stopover

## Crestfield Hotel, 2-4 Crestfield St.

My London hotel needed to be cheap and within walking distance to Kings Cross and St. Pancras Stations. The Crestfield Hotel was one of a number of converted residences near the train stations that offered exactly these features. It had a warren of stairs, leading every which way. It was a tetras puzzle of landings, constructed to maximize the number of rooms.

Room 12A was slightly larger than my QM2 balcony and well designed in its compact efficiency. The twin bed fit snugly in a bay. A four-inch ledge overhanging the mattress as a perfectly adequate bedside table. The adjustable headboard reading light was better than what many hotels offer. It was an en suite room, meaning it had its own toilet and shower, which is not to be taken for granted in this type of hotel. Every day, complimentary cookies, coffee, and both sparkling and still water were left in the room.

Note the luggage storage lit up under the bed.

A generous buffet provided not only a hearty breakfast, but the opportunity to sneak some bread and cheese back to the room for dinner. Hungry students and I must have had the same budget. Many of them also took advantage of this opportunity.

It was perfect for my ten-night stay.

The hotel entrance

Daily complimentary coffee, tea, and snacks were left on the twelve-inch-deep desk.

# Light, Shadow, and the Blackest Black

Before I left Santa Fe, I was lucky to snag a ticket to the National Gallery's special exhibit *Leonardo: Experience a Masterpiece*, which was extended by a coupe of weeks into late January. This immersive blockbuster extravaganza focused on a single painting, Leonardo's masterpiece, the *Virgin of the Rocks*. The exhibit was divided into four spaces, each exploring different themes: the Mind of Leonardo; The Studio; the Light and Shadow Experiment; and the Imagined Chapel.

Now, I know I can be an overly critical person. But this exhibit, at best, lost sight of its raison d'entre. By the end, I wanted to slap both the curator and designer. Metaphorically speaking. Mostly.

The London National Gallery

The exhibition was dominated by technical tricks. The most unsuccessful was in The Studio where a holograph of a woman posing as Mona Lisa was unconvincing an rather creepy. Much more successful were the light and shadow boxes in the Light and Shadow Experiment where different objects were set in the wall. The dark cubicles were surrounded by lights controlled by levers, which acted like dimmer switches. Move one lever up or down and the shadows of the objects changed. Move another lever, change the light again. Move both levers together, change the light. A dozen levers meant there were practically infinite variations on light and shadow. Fun and educational!

Leaving the Light and Shadow Experiment seemed to deposit visitors back at the entrance. Where was the masterpiece we were supposed to experience? I asked a guard where *The Virgin of the Rocks* was displayed. The guard assured me the painting was around a corner. She added that I was not the first to ask.

There it was. The restored masterpiece, *The Virgin of the Rocks*. Though it was hard to tell. The explanation on the wall stated:

> At the end of your journey, you will come face to face
> with the original masterpiece where it hangs on the walls
> of an imagined chapel for you to contemplate how *The
> Virgin of the Rocks* might have appeared in its original
> setting as part of an elaborate altarpiece.

Surrounding the painting was a looping sequence of projections creating a supposed illustration of the lost altar setting where The Virgin of the Rocks supposedly hung. Every minute the images around Leonardo's masterpiece would fade in and out. The shallow room was darkly lit to showcase the projected images. The star of the exhibition had been downgraded to a slideshow.

While I appreciate understanding the context of a work of art, this context so overshadowed the work, it defeated its purpose of allowing visitors to experience the masterpiece. It would have been a simple matter to project a digital image of The Virgin of the Rocks within the imagined altar piece and to display the painting in a room of its own designed to showcase it alone.

Frustrated, I left feeling that I had experienced a curator's indulgence in a technological fun house. Leonardo's masterpiece served only as a pretext for the digital extravaganza.

But, it did get me thinking about light and shadow.

Leonardo wrote:

> The beginnings and ends of shadow lie between the light and darkness and may be infinitely diminished and infinitely increased. Shadow is the means by which bodies display their form. The forms of bodies could not be understood in detail but for shadow.

If shadow is infinitely increased into darkness, then there is no form. Infinite shadow creates the blackest black. The blackest black is a void, absorbing all light.

The blackest black. How could one paint that? True black, I've been told, is the absence of all color. All paint has pigment. All pigment is composed of some color. And all paint has some sort of sheen, from glossy to matte. Even the least bit of shine reflects some light. The blackest black can have no color and has to be the matte-iest of mattes. It seems impossible.

Enter a British technology company, Surrey NanoSystems. It developed a paint called Vantablack in conjunction with some non-artistic project. Vantablack absorbs something like 99.96% of visible light using carbon nanotubes stacked in parallel rows. The energy in the light is turned into heat and dissipated. It's the dark stuff of science. Really, really dark.

Enter Anish Kapoor, creator of Chicago's Cloud Gate (a/k/a The Bean) fame. He's a big, big deal in the contemporary art scene. He has a knighthood. Nobody messes with Anish Kapoor. He obtained the exclusive rights to use Vantablack in art. This pissed off a lot of other, much less famous, much less rich, artists.

Enter Stuart Semple. Semple is a younger British artist. He is far from rich. He does not have a knighthood. He has mixed his own colors and paints since he was at university. He was offended that Kapoor sucked up Vantablack for his exclusive use. Semple had been working on an ultra-fluorescent pink pigment and decided to sell the "pinkest pink," on his website with the following cheeky note:

> By adding this product to your cart, you confirm that you are not Anish Kapoor, you are in no way affiliated to Anish Kapoor, you are not purchasing this item on behalf of Anish Kapoor or an associate of Anish Kapoor. To the best of your knowledge, information, and belief this material will not make its way into the hands of Anish Kapoor.

Kapoor took the bait and got his hands on some of the pinkest pink, posting a photo on Instagram of his extended middle finger dipped in the pink powder.

The game was on. The next level of play? Developing the blackest black to be made available to the humble masses.

After soliciting expertise from artists around the world who supported his #sharetheblack movement, Semple developed several, ever improving, versions of an acrylic "blackest black" paint, BLK 3.0. Semple's creation compares favorably with Vantablack in its opacity and easily outperforms it in availability and user friendliness. The website for BLK 3.0 boasts:

- Absorbs up to 99% of visible light
- Apply with a brush or a spray
- Works with most surfaces
  (wood, paper, canvas, plastic, metal, plaster etc…)
- Thins with water
- Lightfast and archival
- No need for cooking, vacuum chambers,
  or weapons-grade scientists
- Smells like fresh coffee
- Not available to Kapoor

This was all too much fun. I had to get in on the act.

Enter Carol Couch. She is not an artist. She is not rich or famous. She does not have a knighthood. She knows nothing about mixing paint. But she does have a credit card and internet access and knows a bit of fun when she sees it. She ordered BLK 3.0.

To date, Kapoor has only used Vantablack once, on the watch face of the limited edition of ten *Sequential One S110 Evo Vantablack* wristwatches, retailing at $95,000. What's the fun of that?

## Places of Worship

I hadn't planned to go inside St. Paul's Cathedral. My plan was to go by and pay homage to the Disney film *Mary Poppins* by pausing at the steps of the cathedral where the sweet, little old lady sits while Julie Andrews sings *Feed the Birds*.

Yes, I'd read all the blah-di-ditty-blah about how magnificent the cathedral is and how it's all so historically significant, etc. etc. etc.

There has been a church on this site, the highest point in London, since 604. The present English Baroque building is considered to be Sir Christopher Wren's masterpiece. It was completed in 1710 after the old Gothic cathedral, which had been a center of medieval and early modern London life, was destroyed in the Great Fire of 1666. It survived the Blitz, despite direct bomb hits in 1940 and 1941. In more recent memory, Prince Charles and Lady Diana Spencer married there in 1981, and it was the site for the Silver, Gold, and Diamond Jubilee services for Queen Elizabeth II.

Yeah, okay. Whatever. I knew what was important. Julie Andrews singing *Feed the Birds*. For heaven's sake.

I walked over Millennial Bridge which revealed the grand cathedral bit by bit, just as the sun was getting low and the cathedral's bells were chiming. And chiming and chiming. My goodness, I thought, that's a lot of chiming. Like the crescendo of a musical movie score.

As I approached the cathedral, I saw a sign that the Epiphany Carol Service was beginning in about ten minutes. Well, that was fortuitous.

St. Paul's Cathedral and the Millennium Bridge

Several other tourists and I went undercover as faux congregants without entrance tickets. We shuffled through the usual security, took the service pamphlet, and sat down under the immense dome along with the true congregants.

Well, all the blah-di-ditty-blah was absolutely correct, although the cathedral's impressive history was overshadowed by the magnificent of the building itself.  The sheer size was breathtaking, but what dazzled me most were the intricate mosaics above the altar. Jaw droppingly gorgeous.

St. Paul's  interior

As I gazed toward the heavens, trying to keep my jaw closed, angelic singing descended. No choir was in sight. Only heavenly voices enveloping the magnificent dome and the congregants below. The effect evoked raw emotion and a spiritual awe that I have rarely experienced. Perhaps for the first time, I appreciated awe-inspiring cathedrals in their spiritual, rather than secular, incarnation.

Then the service began. Pomp and ritual have their place, even if the choir's entrance broke the spell of divine wonderment. Being a guest at the service, I joined in where appropriate and was respectfully silent otherwise, resisting the temptation to crane my neck and gawk.

The service involved a lot of standing during many prayers and unfamiliar hymns. Then, the congregation rose and followed the priest, first to a suspended, five-foot tall, Greek Orthodox icon, then to the Baptismal Font. There was much standing in a crowd with more prayers and singing.

By this late hour of the day, my arthritic back and hips were pretty painful, and all I could think of was sitting down. Eventually, I maneuvered toward a discrete chair at the edge of the crowd. With enough of a hobble in my walk to appease the somber, seemingly judgmental gaze of the Wands-men and Stewards, who had been ushering the congregation from place to place, I parked myself down until it was time for us all to return to the nave.

Eventually, the service blessedly ended. After some searching, I found a bus back to my hotel, doing my best to hold on to those moments of transcendence.

Inspired by my experience at St. Paul's Cathedral, I decided to attend matins at Westminster Abbey, sung by their boys' choir. I had visions of celestial harmonies filling the Gothic expanse where people had worshipped since the time of Henry III in the mid-13th century.

Alas. The one night that the choir was singing during my stay was cold, rainy, blustery, and dark, of course. The rush hour crush on the Underground was another deterrent. Nevertheless, this was my one chance and I started off from the hotel with the driving rain and the hood of my waterproof rain jacket nearly obscuring my vision.

I made it halfway to Kings Cross Station. A block before I had passed a well-lit McDonald's. It dinnertime. Human weakness overtook me, and I turned around. Soon, I was back at the hotel clutching a soaking bag containing a quarter-pounder with cheese, French fries, and a chocolate shake. (Bad tourist. Bad.)

More than spiritual sustenance, more than aesthetic awe, that night I just wanted convenient comfort food enjoyed in the sanctity of my tiny twin bed.

Sometimes, less exalted golden arches are the most heaven sent.

# Tea for One

High tea is a full meal with meat, fish or eggs, bread, a dessert and, yes, tea. It is eaten from a "high" table, which is to say a regular dining table at the end of the workday. It is a meal of the working classes.

Afternoon tea is the one with the scones, clotted cream, preserves, finger sandwiches, and tiny dessert cakes. And, yes, tea. It was historically served on a "low" table, like a coffee table, between four and five in the afternoon. It is not meant to be a full meal but is intended only to tide one over between lunch and a fashionably late dinner. Definitely high class, even if the tables were low.

Supposedly, it started with Anna, the seventh Duchess of Bedford, who would get peckish between lunch and her dinner served at eight o'clock. In 1840, she asked that a tray of tea, bread and butter be brought up to her room. A grumbling stomach was the humble beginning for such a luxurious tradition.

Anyway. London. Classic, elegant, Afternoon Tea. It was high on my bucket list of London experiences.

So many choices!

*Brown's Hotel* – a favorite of Queen Victoria; tea is served in a dedicated wood-paneled English Tea Room with armchairs, a fireplace, and a menu so extensive it is labelled a library. (33 Albemarle Street, £55)

*Fortnum & Mason* – on the fourth floor of the iconic tea shop, with perhaps, not surprisingly, the widest selection of teas. (181 Piccadilly Street, £60)

*The Dorchester* – served in the Promenade five times a day with extra cushy chairs. Some say the prettiest Afternoon Tea in London. (35 Park Lane, £65)

*The Wolseley* – classic, opulent Mayfair hotel where tea is served in the grande-dame dining room. (160 Piccadilly Street, £30)

*The Ritz* – sumptuously served in its gold gilded, mirrored palm room. Served on a non-traditional 11:30 a.m. to 7:30 p.m. schedule with five sittings and a definite time to vacate your table. (150 Piccadilly, £58)

*The Lanesborough* – served in the lavish Céleste Restaurant across from Buckingham Palace. (Hyde Park Corner, £53)

*The Landmark* – served in the Winter Garden, a five-story atrium with palm trees and piano music in a Grade II Victorian railway hotel. (222 Marylebone Road, £52)

*The Savoy* – served in the Thames Foyer, though you can't see the Thames from the Foyer. Renowned for its impeccable liveried service. (The Strand, £75)

*The Langham* – served in the Palm Court. The first London hotel to serve Afternoon Tea, back in 1865. (1C Portland Place, Regent Street, £62)

*Goring Hotel* – fit for royalty. The Duchess of Cambridge stayed here the night before her wedding and Queen Elizabeth II had her annual staff Christmas lunches here. It is the only hotel to hold a Royal Warrant from HM The Queen for hospitality services. (15 Beeston Place, £50)

*Claridge's* – as classic as it gets in one of London's most elegant hotels. Two sittings of early and late afternoon tea in either the Foyer or more intimate Reading Room. (41 - 43 Brook Street, £70)

This list is just a starting point. There are dozens more options, including contemporary takes on Afternoon Tea and more relaxed, less expensive choices. Each of the venues have tantalizing websites with lavish photos, detailed descriptions of the menus, and other useful information. For instance, both Browns Hotel's and Fortnum & Mason's will refill your plates and generously offer take-home boxes. The Ritz, on the other hand, has reservations with both beginning and ending times, which seems contrary to the point of a leisurely afternoon.

After hours of detailed research, I decided my top three choices were Fortnum & Mason, Brown's Hotel, or Claridge's. Or maybe the Landmark. Or the Savoy. I imagined myself sitting down, choosing my tea, being served the scones and sandwiches and cake tier. Savoring the surroundings. But . . . somehow not. Something was off. Something was missing.

A friend. Conversation. Unlike having coffee solo in a café, Afternoon Tea is meant to be shared. A book or a notebook and pen are de rigueur for cafés. Perhaps because Afternoon Teas was traditionally served on low tables, pulling out a book or a notebook and while being served tiers of delicacies would just be WRONG.

With a sigh, Afternoon Tea was struck from the itinerary.

But, then . . .

On my last day in London, I happened to visit St. Martin-in-the-Fields church.

UNTO
DEATH
FORTITUDE    DEVOTION

It is a sweet church, famous for its concerts, situated near the National Gallery. I was attracted to it because of its many posters welcoming the homeless and offering job training and other services. It explained that it believed those who were facing adversity were closest to God's heart. There was not an admission ticket office or security line. A service was just ending, and the minister waved me in with a warm smile. I wandered in to take a look, lit a candle, and said a prayer when my stomach reminded me that it was lunchtime.

St. Martin's has a "Café in the Crypt" that supports their various missions. Perfect. On my way to the cafeteria, I passed the gift shop. I stopped short at a sign advertising a special combination of Afternoon Tea and a brass rubbing.

Excuse me? Yes, said the cashier. You get the scone, clotted cream, jam, sandwiches, cakes and tea, plus a mini-tutorial on making your own brass rubbing from templates on a nearby wall.

Well, well, well. Well. High Tea in a church's crypt. A coloring book activity to substitute for conversation. Who knew something so high class as Afternoon Tea needed to be paired with children's playtime?

It was too early for tea, which was only served after lunch, but I could get started on the brass rubbing. Brass rubbings take a surprising amount of muscle, much harder than coloring with crayons. Good thing I had Afternoon Tea for sustenance.

It wasn't particularly elegant. I ordered from the buffet line. It took two trips to my worktable to carry out my tiers of cakes and sandwiches, and my tea, of course. After two hours, with a sore right arm, I dusted off my hands, bussed my empty dishes to the dirty dish trolley, rolled up my completed brass rubbing, and went on my way, giggling like a little kid.

St. Martin-in-the-Fields Church (opposite page)

The work in progress. Inscribed on the back of the template:
Sir Thomas and Lady Margaret Beauchamp, Warwick, 1406 (opposite page)

# London Transportation

My favorite mode of transportation in London was to float along the Thames on the hop-on-hop-off Thames Clippers (now Uber Boat by Thames Clippers). They ply London's oldest highway, the River Thames, which cuts through the heart of London. They offered unique views of the London skyline, hitting all the highlights from Parliament to the London Eye, Tower Bridge, and Greenwich. Protected from the wind and chill of London's misty winter weather, with hot cocoa, beer, wine, cocktails, and sandwiches available for purchase, it seemed the only way to travel. Their regular schedule, however, is intended primarily for commuters and their stops are dictated by the location of piers.

If the Clippers do not meet your transportation needs, London, fortunately, has plenty of other options. Walking. Cycling. Black cabs. The Underground. Double-decker buses. London has something for everyone.

Bicycles for rent

London Underground

A crowd waiting to enter the Oxford Street Underground Station

A street view from the upper level of a double-decker bus

# Route Map

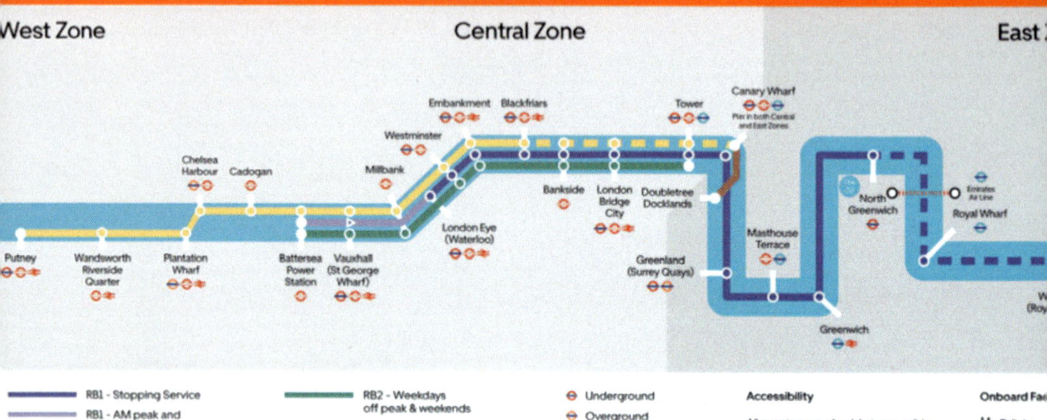


The Thames Clippers route map

A Thames Clipper docking

The interior of a Thames Clipper with the Elizabeth Tower and Big Ben under renovation

The London Skyline view from the Thames Clipper

citycru
MILLENNIUM CIT
LONDON

## Where am I?

I was in Greenwich, about to cross from the Western to the Eastern Hemisphere. I was heading up a hill in search of the Royal Observatory Greenwich, seeking the line that delineates East from West. The line where time begins at zero. The line that tells us where we are, with the satisfying longitudinal measurement of 0°0'0". The Greenwich Prime Meridian that defines Greenwich Mean Time.

The London skyline from the Royal Observatory Greenwich.

The Observatory was founded in 1675 by King Charles II. It moved to East Sussex in 1947 because of light pollution from London, then to Cambridge in 1990. The Greenwich site is now under the care of the National Maritime Museum.

The Prime Meridian could be anywhere in the world. But the Royal Observatory Greenwich had been busy for centuries, charting the sky and setting the baseline for time and place. By 1884, when the Greenwich Meridian was chosen as the international Prime Meridian. Seventy-three percent of the world's commerce used sea charts based on the Greenwich Meridian.

The sea charts were critical. Though set on land and looking toward the sky, the Greenwich Meridian and Royal Observatory were all about the sea.

Here's the deal. Anytime you want to get somewhere, you have to start somewhere. On land, landmarks, as their name implies, mark where you are on land. But, in the middle of the ocean, you are literally "at sea," with no landmarks to tell you where you are.

Humans, of course, have long been navigating vast bodies of water. For thousands of years, the Polynesians used the stars, cloud formations, wind patterns, and sea swells to sail the Pacific. Europeans depended far more on measurements and math. They depended on knowing their longitude and latitude.

A ship's north/south position, its latitude, is determined by measuring the angle of the horizon of the sun or the North Star and applying simple arithmetic. Locating longitude, a ship's east/west position, is far, far more, complicated. It requires knowing the precise locations of numerous stars on any given night of the year, taking measurements, then applying a set of trigonometric equations to those measurements.

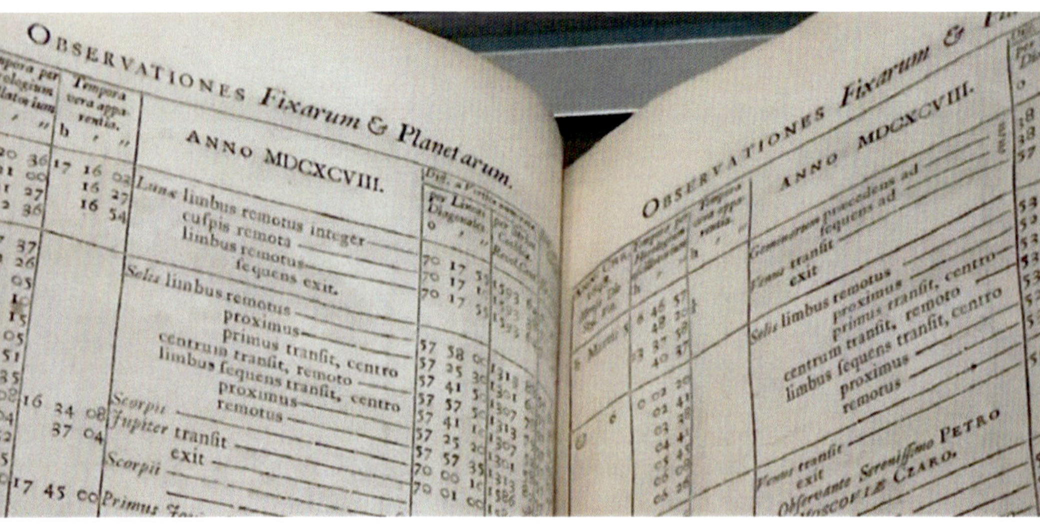

A book of star charts
John Flamsteed, appointed as the First Royal Astronomer in 1675, spent forty years recording the exact time and altitude of each star as it crossed the meridian line.

Celestial navigation is quite accurate and still used today. It does, however, have limitations. Like cloudy skies. It doesn't take too many nights of cloudy skies for a ship to veer dangerously off course. An alternative was needed. A measurement that didn't depend on what the eye could observe. Time.

Happily, natural measurements of space and time neatly correlate with one another. The circumference of the earth and the length of a day are quite compatible, mathematically speaking.

A day can be divided into roughly twenty-four hours. The earth's circumference is roughly 360 degrees. Let's say we divide the earth into imaginary lines running between the North and South Poles. Let's call these lines meridians. If we happen to draw 24 equidistant meridians, the space between them is 15 degrees of the Earth's circumference. This is because 360 degrees divided by 24 hours equals 15 degrees. Another neat formula is that the 1,440 seconds of a day divided by 360 degrees equals 4 degrees.

This means that each hour of the day corresponds to fifteen degrees longitudinal distance. Each minute of the day corresponds to four degrees longitude. The difference in time allows you to calculate the distance between east and west.

For example, the QM2 is sailing from Southampton to New York. After a few days at sea, we might wonder how far west we have traveled. It is 8 a.m. onboard. If we know that it is noon in Southampton, a four-hour difference, we know we have traveled sixty degrees west. We know where we are.

With today's technology, it is a simple matter to know the current time of a distant place. Just check the internet or take a watch or clock onboard and keep it set to the time of the place you want to track. But back in the day, they didn't have the internet and they didn't have clocks that could maintain a constant time at sea.

They had accurate clocks on land. The pendulum clock was invented in the mid-1600s and continued to be the most advance timekeeping technology until the quartz clock was invented in the 1940s. Pendulum clocks, however, are useless in choppy waters or when subjected to changes in temperature, humidity, or even barometric pressure. What was needed was a sea clock.

Britain especially needed a sea clock as it began to engage in global trade and establish far flung colonies. In 1714, after too many shipwrecks, the English Parliament passed the Longitude Act. This Act set up a competition for the invention of a simple, practical, and precise sea clock. It took decades to find a sufficient solution.

In the end, John Harrison was the man of the hour. Or rather the man of 2.6666 seconds. This is how much time his H4 clock lost per day on a voyage between England and Barbados in 1764. The H4, which is about the size of a large pocket watch, was not only accurate and portable, but, as importantly, reproducible.

John Harrison posing with H4.

Time and technology marched on. Today, atomic clocks lose only one second every fifteen billion years.

One hundred years after the adoption of the Greenwich Prime Meridian as the Prime Meridian, it was displaced by the IERS Reference Meridian (IRM) as the international standard. The IRM uses lunar and satellite laser ranging and very-long-baseline interferometry to determine a plane that passes through the earth's center mass. This plane establishes the longitudinal line for the IRM. It is about 334 feet east of the Greenwich Meridian line. With these advances, the brass Greenwich Meridian Line embedded in the earth became a scientific anachronism even as it gained popularity as a tourist hotspot.

One can't stand over the IRM, straddling the Eastern and Western Hemispheres like one can the Greenwich Meridian. It has no permanent marker and shifts by infinitesimal degrees as as the earth's tectonic plates move ever so slightly. The quest for precision will always be at odds with the quest for fixity. The more we know, the less certain we are as to exactly where, or even when, we are.

This is all the more true after physicists thought up spacetime. Spacetime melds space and time. It as been described as the fusion of the three dimensions of space and the one dimension of time into a single fourth dimensional manifold, where positions are known as events.

The truth is, we all exist somewhere between space and time. Some place where land, sea, and sky converge. Some place where every moment of our lives is an event.

Bogota 74° 03' W
Quito 78° 32' W
Lima 77° 03' W
St Helena 5° 43' W
La Paz 68° 10' W
Brasilia 47° 40' W
Tahiti 149° 34' W
Accra 00° W
Hong Kong E
Hanoi 105° E
Rangoon 96° E
Bangkok 100° E
Saigon 106° E
Addis Ababa 38° E
Bombay 72° E
Colombo 79° E
Lagos 3° E
Kuala Lumpur 101° E
Singapore 103° 48' E
Nairobi 36° 50' E
Jakarta 106° 45' E



The Greenwich Meridian Line

# Crossing the English Channel

The Eurostar high speed passenger train is the most convenient way to get from central London to central Paris. When booking my ticket, I was most excited about the idea of passing through the Chunnel.

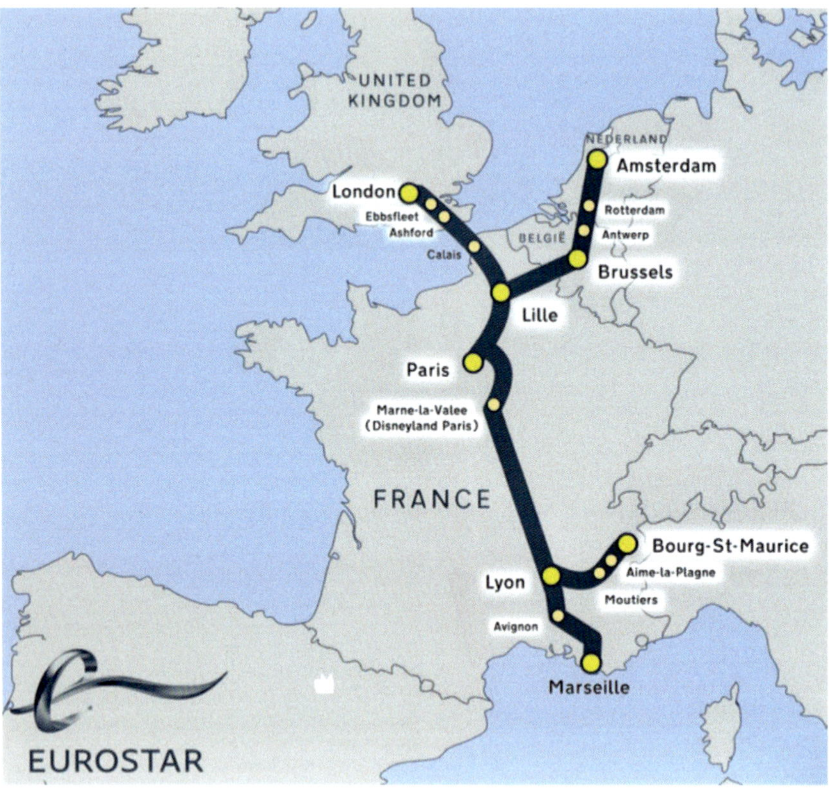


The Chunnel is the affectionate name for the tunnel that runs beneath the English Channel. It lies 377 feet below sea level and 246 feet below the seabed at its lowest point. It runs underwater for twenty-three miles. It was the closest I would come to taking a submarine on this trip. Okay, that's a stretch. But, as you know by now, I like to pretend.

I settled into my window seat after boarding at St. Pancras Station in London. I didn't want to miss a thing. I certainly didn't want to miss the Chunnel. I diligently watched the scenery rush by. And when I say rush, I mean really, really rush. The countryside was hardly visible at speeds up to 186 miles per hour. When we went through various tunnels shortly after leaving London, however, the only thing visible was my static reflection in the glass.

The total trip takes just over two hours, so, after about half an hour, I began to think each new tunnel might be the Chunnel. Not to be deterred by watching only my own face, my mind raced. Was this the Chunnel? Were we under the English Channel now? Or now? Was this it? All the tunnels seemed the same, just my face looking back at me, vainly straining to discern something that would indicate we were under the English Channel.

Then, suddenly, we were in the French countryside. Where had the Chunnel gone?  Hardly before I was able to register my disappointment, we were disembarking at Gare du Nord in Paris.

The Chunnel is an amazing feat of engineering. The most amazing thing about the Chunnel, however, is how they managed to make it disappear.

St. Pancras International Train Station, London

Eurostar trains in Gare du Nord

# PART III
## Paris

2020

# Paris

January 16 to April 9, 2020

# Carol's City of Lights

Paris is never far away.

My sister Barbara painted me a fantasy Paris complete with my own fantasy garret apartment. She titled it *Carol's City of Lights*. The painting

*Carol's City of Lights* by B. Couch (2014)

hangs above my bed in Santa Fe, yet gives me a view of my imaginary Paris apartment that Barbara thoughtfully painted into the cityscape. It is the second building from the left, top floor, if you ever want to stop by.

## 25 blvd dé Sébastopol, 1st arr.
Métro: Châtelet/Les Halles (Lines 1, 4, 7, 11 and 14)
RER: (Lines A, B and D)

The fantasy garret apartment Barbara painted became more real during my 2020 three-month stay. My apartment was on the 6th and top floor.

I had a love/hate relationship with the apartment.

Early morning view from the living room windows

The Fountain of the Innocents is in the center of the Place Joachim-du-Bellay. Saint Eustache church is on the horizon to the right. The modern Westfield Shopping Mall, which sits above the transportation hub of Châtelet/Les Halles, peeks between Place Joachim-du-Bellay and St. Eustache Church.

View from the hallway's garret window

On the one hand, there was plenty to kvetch about. The kitchen was less than clean. The ice in the freezer was so thick that the door would not close. A jumble of unusable electronics obscured the WIFI router, which wasn't working. The mattress extruded so much fluff that I was in danger of sleeping on bare bed slats. The laundry room was cluttered ceiling to floor, burying the clothes washer and wall vents labeled, "DO NOT COVER." All of the IKEA furniture, most especially the couch, was well beyond its "best by" date.

It usually takes me a few days to nest in a new place. This place took an intensive week of cleaning and organizing just to feel functional. Then, just as the apartment was in order, the elevator went out of order. I suppose once you get used to it, walking up six flights is good exercise.

A cheery start to the climb

The teeny, tiny elevator, typical of retrofitted Hausmann buildings

A view from the living room window

One of the apartment's two air shafts

On the plus side, the apartment afforded me an ongoing narrative of the buskers, demonstrators, construction workers, commuters, street people, delivery cyclists, shoppers, and those who nightly set up tents in the shop fronts as their homes in the Place Joachim-du-Bellay. The air shafts gave glimpses of the neighbors' lives.

I was able to check weather updates and observe the evolution of the seasons from late winter to early spring through its many windows.

For all its faults and frustrations, the apartment had plenty to love.

# Eats

I like food well enough, but I'm not a foodie. When I consider where to eat, I look first at the ambience and only secondarily at the menu.

There are a few things that are helpful to know about eating out in France. For instance, why are some places called restaurants, others bistros, and yet others brasseries? Where do cafés fit in?

A basic guide:

*Brasseries* originally meant breweries and their fare, generally available from morning until late night, is traditionally French, which is to say steak tartare, coq au vin, steak frites, choucroute garnie (braised sauerkraut with mixed meats), and mussels.

*Bistros* are known for their quick* service and tend to close between the lunch and dinner hours. Their menus are similar to brasseries, but often more limited, emphasizing simpler dishes. Like the menu, the ambience tends to be more casual than brasseries.

*Restaurants* offer a wide variety of cuisines from around the world. Paris reportedly has over 40,000 restaurants, so the variety is nearly unlimited. Like bistros, restaurants tend to close between lunch and dinner. They vary between the inexpensive to those where you will need to mortgage your home for a night out.

*Cafés* are all about drinking, alcoholic and not, and are open from early morning to late night. Basic food like a croque monsieur, cheese plates, salads, and sandwiches are available, but lingering and conviviality are emphasized rather than food. Ordering just a coffee or a glass of wine is acceptable unless a table is set with a placemat, usually during regular meal hours. If you sit at one of these tables, you are expected to order food.

* relatively speaking - US tourists should not expect a "quick bite" at any traditional French eatery.

A typical sidewalk menu board offers French onion soup, salads, bœuf tartare, duck breast and pasta. The Sarah Bernhardt brasserie also offers a typical American hamburger, which was far better than anything the ubiquitous McDonald's or Burger King have to offer.

What makes the Sarah Bernhardt a brasserie rather than a bistro is its opening hours, from 7 a.m. until midnight. Signs saying "service continu," indicate a brasserie or restaurant, offering continuous service from breakfast or lunch through dinner.

These distinctions might be academic, however. It is easiest just to check the menu in front of where you are thinking of eating and not to be surprised if a place is closed between meals.

Street food is always an option. One of my go-to meals was from a crêperie stand around the corner from my apartment. It offered sweet and savory crêpes and more than one night found me at home with a ham and cheese crêpe followed by a Nutella crêpe for dessert.

Then, there is the classic French picnic of a baguette, cheese, fruit, and a bottle of wine. The banks of the Seine or a grassy knoll in one of the many parks are perfect settings to feel like you are in a romance movie set in Paris, even if dining solo.

The most memorable meal I had was when my friend Lynn suggested we eat at L'Escargot Montorgueil, a short walk from the apartment. Seduced by the Belle Epoque decor and feeling I should try the house specialities, I ordered snails and frog legs.

Some people disparage frog legs as tasting like chicken legs, only with less meat. I must disagree. As a non-foodie, I don't have the vocabulary to describe the taste of frog legs at L'Escargot, but they were uniquely delicious and I would certainly go back for more.

UNESCO has designated French cuisine a world intangible heritage. Any place that can get me to try and enjoy frog legs is is indeed worthy of special recognition.

Tourist Tip on Tips: Most guidebooks will tell you that tips are not expected in France when dining out. Back in the day, when cash was used to pay the bill, any coins returned as change would be left on the table. Paying by credit card is now the norm and there are options on the receipt for tips. I have found that tips are always appreciated.

# Sans Domicile Fixe

The most disturbing part of my time in Paris was, by far, the large number of unhoused people. In France, they are sans domicile fixe (without a fixed residence).

A few of those who were sans domicile fixe became familiar. The old woman who methodically set up her green tent in the same breezeway every night. The angry young woman who would shout at the police when they told her every morning that she and her two dogs had to move out of the shopfront so it could open. The man who carried two bags and sat patiently forlorn for hours next to the Fountain of the Innocents.

Others were ghostly presences. Bedding was stashed in the crevice of a shop front. A cardboard windbreak was propped in Shake 'n Steak's entrance. Those with regular spots where they asked for food or money or simply sat dejected, waiting out the day.

I began to keep euro coins handy to give out. Once I gave a young boy the pastry I had just bought. I took a list of hygiene products that the city's Protection Civile passed out at a grocery entrance and filled my handbasket to give them on my way out.

It wasn't enough. It could never be enough.

# Rebuilding Notre Dame

"Your poor Notre Dame!" was the first inkling I had of the fire on April 15, 2019. My sister had sent an email. I immediately started searching the internet. It didn't take long for me to watch, in horror, with hundreds of thousands of others, as the fire billowed smoke and the spire collapsed. We watched, straining with hope, some of us praying, that the towers and walls would stand, that the rose stained-glass windows would somehow survive the heat.

The towers and walls did stand. The rose windows, in fact, all of the stained glass, was miraculously undamaged except for a covering of toxic ash that spread throughout the entire area as the lead roof burned. Holy relics and much of the artwork were passed hand-to-hand out of danger by a human chain of firefighters, other first responders, and volunteers. As bad as it was, it could have been worse. Much, much worse.

Before the fire

While the cause of the fire is not known, it was probably sparked by faulty electrical wiring being used for repairs already underway. To the outside observer, Notre Dame may have looked magnificent with its newly cleaned interior and western façade, but the spire's wooden frame had been rotting from leaks in its lead roof and rain and pollution had weakened the exterior stone.

In 2017, André Finot, a spokesperson for the cathedral, was quoted in the *New York Times* as saying, "Everywhere the stone is eroded, and the more the wind blows, the more all of these little pieces keep falling. It's spinning out of control everywhere." Netting had been installed to protect passersby from falling masonry.

After the fire, with the netting and burned scaffolding still in place
from the renovation underway before the fire (February 2020)

The melted scaffolding that had surrounded the spire before the fire


The stained glass was removed for cleaning and repair and the flying buttresses were supported with bespoke wooden frames. The Cathedral would not be fully stabilized until November 2020.

The renovation work falls within the province of the French government as a result of France's long and deeply fraught struggle with the separation of church and state, particularly between the Catholic Church and the state. The history is far too complex to even summarize here but one key event was the passage of the December 9, 1905, Law on the Separation of Church, which put an end to the government funding of religious groups. It also declared that all religious buildings in existence as of that date were the property of the state and local governments, though they would be made available for church purposes.

This state of affairs explains why France's president, Emmanuel Macron, was the one to speak out about the cathedral's future. He rashly asserted, even before the flames were extinguished, that Notre Dame would be rebuilt within five years. A couple of days later, the government announced an international competition to redesign the cathedral's roofline destroyed in the fire. France's prime minister, Édouard Philippe, said the competition would be an opportunity to create "a spire suited to the techniques and challenges of our time."

Philippe went on to say, "The international competition will allow us to ask the question of whether we should even recreate the spire as it was conceived by Viollet-le-Duc. Or, as is often the case in the evolution of heritage, whether we should endow Notre Dame with a new spire. This is obviously a huge challenge, a historic responsibility."

Heritage. Historic responsibility. Modern design. Debate and controversy were instantly ignited.

The cathedral's chief architect, Philippe Villeneuve, threatened to resign rather than take part in building a modern spire. In response, the army general Jean-Louis Georgelin, who was overseeing the reconstruction, told Villeneuve to "shut his mouth." This exchange made international news.

The French parliament passed a law governing the reconstruction which included a provision that the restoration must "preserve the historic, artistic and architectural interest of the monument."

The National Heritage and Architecture Commission, an advisory body for restoration projects, urged Macron to adhere to the original design in order to "guarantee the authenticity, the harmony, and the coherence of this masterpiece of Gothic architecture." Public opinion polls indicated 55% of the French people wanted the structure rebuilt as it had been.

In July 2020, Macron, as the final arbiter of the rebuild, ended speculations about the Cathedral's fate and decided that Notre Dame would be restored to its "original" state, including Viollet-le-Duc's spire. The reconstruction was to be à l'identique, down to the toxic lead material in the roof and spire.

The Elysée Palace said Macron's main concern was "not delaying the reconstruction and making it complicated – things had to be cleared up quickly." France, after all, was hosting the 2024 Summer Olympics. And Macron did promise in 2019, as the cathedral burned, that Notre Dame would be rebuilt in five years, which just happened to coincide with the Olympic timetable.

Political cynicism aside, many were relieved. Innovative designs combined with historic buildings are fraught. Perhaps most famously, I.M. Pei's 1989 Louvre pyramid continues to be controversial.

Designs submitted for the reconstruction of Notre Dame offered plenty of justification for skepticism. A comical-if-it-weren't-so-egregious submission for a public swimming pool on the cathedral's roof is perhaps the most notorious. Others included a massive golden spire in the shape of a flame. One suggested a greenhouse.

Yet, some submissions were more thoughtful.

Despite my traditionalist tendencies, I would at least have given some consideration to a design that maintained the silhouette of the destroyed roof and spire but used stained glass in place of the toxic lead. This proposal's use of traditional materials in an unusual way and the dazzling mosaic of light from the stained glass at night seemed sympathetic to the architectural heritage of the cathedral while giving the structure a modern twist. I'm not saying that this is how Notre Dame should have been rebuilt but it offers a glimpse of positive possibilities.

One argument in favor of change is the fact that Notre Dame's architecture has never been static. The Cathedral has undergone numerous revisions throughout the centuries, reflecting changes in aesthetic tastes and the introduction of modern materials and construction methods.

It's hard to imagine but the stone façade we are all so familiar with had been painted until 1486. The medieval roof had been constructed of black, gold, red and green tiles before they were replaced with lead. The original walls were demolished in the 13th century before construction was even finished in order to install larger windows, including the iconic rose windows. The side chapels were not part of the original design, and many continue to lament how they darken the interior and break up the vertical lines of the buttresses.

Electricity replaced manually ringing the bells in 1955. Parts of the great organ have been computerized.

During the reign of Louis XIV, in the 18th century, many of the original stained-glass windows were replaced with clear glass. Except for the three rose windows, all of the stained glass we now see is "new." The original rood screen, an ornate partition between the choir and nave, was pulled down at the same time. Then, Louis XIV wanted an opening large enough for processional carriages to pass through. Down went a pillar of the central doorway.

In the 19th century, a major restoration by Eugène Viollet-le-Duc was undertaken. The spire that burned in April 2019 was not the original spire constructed in the 13th century. That spire had been removed in 1786 after the wind weakened and bent it over the centuries. Viollet-le-Duc replaced the fallen spire with one that was taller and more ornate than the original. He said he wanted to build what he thought the spire should look like, not what the spire had looked like before.

Many of the gargoyles and chimeras that seem like they have been there since medieval times were added during this restoration, again in keeping with Viollet-le-Duc's conception of what the Cathedral should look like. No small part of what we have come to love and admire about Notre Dame is his 19th century handiwork.

As Robert Zaretsky wrote in an August 2020 article in *Foreign Affairs*, "Notre Dame has become a site where lay people see a past that never was, and professionals see a past that always was in one man's [Viollet-le-Duc's] imagination." It is that imaginary past created by centuries of change that will be recreated in this latest restoration.

Certainly, a restoration that is à l'identique to what existed immediately before the fire is the safest course of action (except for replacing the lead). And I am not one to say it is necessarily the wrong course of action, but it does erase the catastrophic 2019 fire, which I believe should be commemorated in a substantial way. By rebuilding à l'identique, the 21st century will be more obscure than the 12th or 18th.

Yet, I suppose, this is itself a reflection of these times. The very absence of change is a testament to the current longing for stability, to an exhaustion from adjusting to too many changes and challenges. In the midst of a global pandemic, social unrest, personal upheaval, financial crises, technological threats, and political turmoil, it is not surprising that we opt for what is familiar, what seems safely immutable.

 Spring 2023, as the scaffolding rises to rebuild the tower

Perhaps, in these turbulent days, preserving our sense of the past, no matter how inadequate or inaccurate, is the only way we can manage the strength to face the future.

Note: Notre Dame reopened to the public on December 7, 2024. The first public mass since the fire was celebrated on December 8, 2024.

# Ballooning Philosophies

Philosophizing is embedded in the French psyche, and it is contagious.

Out and about one day, doing nothing in particular, I passed by a trash bin near Les Halles. A whale was suspended on an orange balloon that floated above the garbage.

I had to stop. The fate of this whale raised all sorts of questions. Who put it there and why? How can it look so curious and content after being tossed aside? What are the necessary conditions for happiness? Does the white stick attached to the balloon connect it to the garbage or keep it separate? What is connection? Why are the bars in front of the whale wrenched open? Do they symbolize the potential for freedom? What is freedom?   What is symbolism?

Just a simple balloon in an ordinary trash bin on a nothing special day. Unless you are in France.

# French Discourse and Discontent

Complaining is the French way of making small talk. Brits talk about the weather. The French complain.

The French also seem to reflexively answer "non" to any question. But the "non" is nuanced. As the French comedian Olivier Giraud, explains, "Answering 'non' gives you the option to say 'oui' later. When you say 'oui', you can no longer say 'non!' We must not forget that the French are a people of protest, and a protest always starts with a 'non'."

If complaining is the French national pastime, protesting is the French national sport.

Protesting is rooted in French history. France's national holiday commemorates the violent protest against monarchical rule by the storming of the Bastille on July 14, 1789. Three months later, thousands of market women marched more than ten miles from Paris to Versailles to protest the price of bread in the midst of widespread famine. (There is no historical evidence that Marie Antionette said, "Let them eat cake." but it fair to say this remark reflected the aristocracy's attitude.)

In the more than two hundred years since the French Revolution, the French people have frequently exercised their right to say "Non!" and to protest social injustices.

     A 1789 illustration of the Women's March on Versailles

The French penchant for protests was on full-blown display when I arrived at Gare du Nord on January 16, 2020, forty-one days into an uninterrupted transportation strike. Few métro or RER lines were running, and taxis could barely keep up with the demand. After more than an hour in line, I got into my taxi, and we began slowly snaking through the congested streets to my apartment. The taxi driver spoke enough English that I could understand his complaints about the strike, about the other taxi drivers, about social deterioration, and, of course, about the French government.

The strike was in opposition to the government's proposed pension reform. Public polling shows the French are generally in favor of pension reform, but the current proposals are perceived as unnecessary. The government argues that increased life expectancy and lower birth rates threaten the solvency of the pension system. Unfortunately for the government, the country's independent Pension Advisory Council told parliament that "pension spending is not out of control – it's relatively contained."

Protesters also objected to the pension plan as both regressive in terms of quality of life and economically unfair. A government administrator admitted that the proposals would penalize women who interrupted paid work to care for children.

The transportation workers were not alone in their protests. The reforms would affect many sectors of the work force and strikes were called by teachers, lawyers, artists, and others, who all felt corporations and those in the highest tax brackets should contribute a larger share to pension solvency.

"Retirement is defensible."

The US State Department runs a Smart Traveler program. If you sign up, you will get regular notifications of scheduled demonstrations with advice about safety precautions you should take. In 2020, I received a notification about a massive protest scheduled for January 24th. One of the main thoroughfares was blvd de Sébastopol. Having seen the bank across the street boarding up its windows, newscasts broadcasting previous violent demonstrations, and darkened vans depositing dozens of police in riot gear in the Place Joachim-du-Bellay, caution easily overrode any curiosity about events, and I tucked in to read a book.

Bank windows across the street from my apartment entrance in 2020

The news media mostly hypes the violence associated with French protests. In fact, most protesters simply want to have their voices peacefully heard through marches and strikes. Too little attention is given to protests with that "je ne sais quoi" of French flair. Ballerinas from the Paris Opéra protested by performed *Swan Lake* in front of the Palais Garnier. Union workers from an electric company strategically cut power to certain companies while restoring power to homes unable to pay their bills in what was called a "Robin Hood operation."

Shortly after the massive January 24th, 2020, demonstrations throughout the country, the government made major concessions. But, before any final agreement was reached, Covid lockdowns put pension reform and opposition demonstrations on the back burner.

By early 2023, however, the government was again pushing pension reform legislation and unions revived the strikes.

One 2023 demonstration march, sponsored by several unions, passed below my window. From the noise, I thought it was a big street party until I looked out the window and saw people dressed in union colors, carrying signs with union logos, singing and dancing along to upbeat music. Someone looked up at the window. I waved. They waved back. It was exhilarating as the parade took more than thirty minutes to pass by.

Banners in front of Paris's city hall in 2023, supporting the strikers

Less pleasant was the three-week strike by sanitation workers in February. As the stench grew along with the piles of trash, I would remind myself that the life expectancy of sanitation workers in Paris is decades shorter than the average. No wonder maintaining an earlier retirement age was vital to them.

When you are in Paris and inevitably confronted with the inconvenience of some sort of strike, the best thing to do is what the Parisians do. Complain and then take it all in stride.

Rue Saint-Germain during the sanitation workers' strike in 2023

A pension protest demonstration below my apartment in 2023 (opposite page)

## Space Invaders

In 1998, tiled or "pixelated" graffiti art began appearing on Paris's streets. The artist styles himself as an Unidentified Free Artist (UFA) with the code name Invader. Taito creatures from the video game Space Invaders were the original inspiration, but the universe of creatures has expanded as far as the imagination can take them.

The geography of the invasion has also expanded, and Space Invaders can now be found from Tunisia to Tokyo, Bhutan to Los Angeles, Hong Kong to New York, and from Morocco to Melbourne. They have landed in the Serengeti desert and dived deep underwater in Cancún Bay. Befitting their name, they have even invaded the International Space Station. They may strike at any time in any place.

Some of the invaders have been obliterated by angry landowners who are hostile to their existence. Some have been stolen for sale on the black market. Each of Invader's original pieces has a single replica, called an Alias, which is authorized for sale. Rare, out-of-print maps and guides to Invader locations sell for thousands of dollars.

The artist Invader, however, recommends an economical way of acquiring his work. Just go to your local home improvement store, buy some tiles, and replicate his designs yourself. Better yet, make up your own.

For myself, I was content to play a street art version of *Where's Waldo?,* keeping a lookout for the little critters.

PARIS
300

6ᵉ Arrᵗ
RUE
DU DRAGON

## The Eiffel Tower

The iconic. The rightly replicated. The most recognizable symbol of Paris.

I gasped at my first distant view of it in 2007. I knew then that I had arrived in Paris. Later, I stood beneath it and stared up at its massive, delicate, elaborate, weighty beauty. I went up the tower at night when its lights dramatized the intricacies of its iron girders, every bolt a punctuation mark. The tower and the view were both magnificent.

Built for the 1889 Exposition Universelle, it was not intended to be the world-renowned landmark it has been become. In fact, it was originally scheduled to be demolished twenty years after it was built.

But popularity and practicality overruled that ill-conceived plan. Over 1,953,000 ticket holders saw it during the Exposition and the crowds have kept coming. Gustave Eiffel also made sure it served strategically important communications and scientific purposes. From the beginning, it served as a weather station and a platform for experiments. In one, a Jesuit priest, Theodor Wulf, discovered cosmic rays in 1910 by measuring the differences in radiation between the top and the bottom of the tower.

Its future was secured after it was used for pioneering radio communications and the French military set up a permanent radio station.

The tower even played a role in setting international time by broadcasting a signal twice a day that was accurate to a fraction of a second. Today, the tower continues its critical role as a communications center with over one-hundred antennae attached to its top.

When it was constructed in 1889, the Eiffel Tower was the largest free-standing structure in the world. At 1,024 feet, it held this record for over forty years until the Chrysler Building in New York was completed in 1930, standing at 1,046 feet. The current record holder is the Burj Khalifa in Dubai that punctures the sky at 2,716 feet. That's over 240 stories. Oxygen masks optional.

Some well-worn statistics are worth repeating:

| | |
|---|---|
| Weight of the metal frame | 7,300 tons |
| Total weight | 10,100 tons |
| Number of rivets | 2.5 million |
| Number of iron parts | 18,038 |
| Number of design drawings | 5,300 |
| Months to construct | 26 |
| Number of workers | 300 |
| Number of deaths | 0* |
| Amount of paint | 60 tons |
| Frequency of repainting | every 7 years |
| Wind gusts at the top | up to 100 mph |
| Visitors per year | 7 million |
| Number of lightbulbs | 20,000 |
| Steps to the top | 1,665 |

* One worker died just before the Tower opened. It was his day off and he was giving his girlfriend an unofficial tour when he lost his footing and fell.

What is most impressive about the Eiffel Tower, however, is hidden within the numbers. As with any tall structure, the greatest engineering challenge is how to counteract the force of wind. The brilliance of the Eiffel Tower's design is to welcome the wind through all of its voids. It harmonizes iron and air and, by doing so, it neutralizes the greatest threat to its stability.

Not everyone was impressed by this design. Initially, the arbiters of high culture objected to the tower in no uncertain terms. Three hundred writers, painters, sculptors, architects, and "lovers of the beauty of Paris" wrote in *Le Temps* that the tower was "a gigantic black factory chimney." There were protests that the tower was "useless and monstrous" and "an odious column of bolted metal."

"The strength of the tower rests in its voids." - unknown

In response, Gustave Eiffel wrote:

> For my part I believe that the Tower will possess its own beauty. Are we to believe that because one is an engineer, one is not preoccupied by beauty in one's constructions, or that one does not seek to create elegance as well as solidity and durability? Is it not true that the very conditions which give strength also conform to the hidden rules of harmony?

Clearly, Eiffel won that debate.

After my ascent up the tower in 2007, I've been back several times. As awe inspiring as the tower itself is, these visits have been disheartening. The problem is the area beneath the tower. It is an unattractive, uninspired concrete expanse where ticket booths and souvenir sales dominate. The park around the tower is little more than a shadeless, downtrodden expanse of patchy grass. Roaring streets confront anyone making their way to the tower from the two closest métro stations.

All of that is about to change, for better and worse. The worse is the installation of security barriers circling the tower's perimeter.

The only nonstructural elements are the decorative scrolls under the arches.

Security throughout Paris was significantly increased after the November 13, 2015, coordinated attacks throughout the city which killed 130 people and injured over 400 more, one hundred of those seriously. It was the deadliest day in Paris since WWII.

Although the tower was not part of these attacks, its symbolic importance and its popularity as a tourist attraction make it a prime target. Unlike the wind, this threat is not one to be welcomed in with voids.

To their credit, the city and SESE, the company that manages the tower, tried to make these barriers as unobtrusive and even as attractive as possible.

The walls on the north and south perimeters made of
state-of-the-art ultra-transparent bulletproof glass.

Still, it feels oppressive. Bollards surround the entire area to prevent bomb-ladened vehicles from getting close to the tower. Opération Sentinelle, a branch of the military, has soldiers patrolling the area with automatic rifles. Though there had been an armed military presence at the tower when I first visited in 2007, these felt more ominous.

The good news is that the security changes prompted a broad rethinking of the entire area to address the overcrowding, the lack of accessibility and amenities, and the dearth of greenery.

The result is a massively ambitious plan to create the largest park in Paris with the Eiffel Tower as the centerpiece.

The Pont d'Iéna, the bridge over the Seine between the Trocadero and the Eiffel Tower, will be transformed into a pedestrian garden. Current bridge traffic will be redirected into a tunnel.

Greenery and water features will replace asphalt and concrete. Two duck ponds will be reconstructed, a small grotto and waterfall will be refurbished, various fountains and tens of thousands of plants and trees will be planted in a creative recreation of the historic landscaping of the area. There will also be a lawned amphitheater and two new pedestrian squares. Historic viewpoints will be recaptured.

There will be more kiosks and ticket offices to reduce lines and a left luggage area will be built. All these commercial enterprises will be sunk into the ground buttressed by raised lawns creating an unobstructed sense of greenery. Though I haven't read anything specific, one has to assume they will also add more, much needed, public toilet facilities.

The first phase, from the Trocadero to the Champs des Mars, is scheduled for completion by 2024, in time for the summer Olympics being hosted by Paris. The second phase, from the Champs des Mars to the Ecole Militaire, should be completed by 2030.

The metal fences installed on the east and west perimeters are designed to mimic the outline of the tower. (opposite page)

Tour Eiffel Entrée 2
Eiffel Tower Entrance 2
Torre Eiffel Entrada 2
艾菲尔铁塔入口2
120m

The $80 million cost to complete the first phase will be entirely covered by proceeds from ticket sales. There will be no cost to enter the gardens below the tower, though people will have to pass through security.

No traffic, increased shade, shorter ticket lines, water features, better amenities and lush gardens. But there is no getting away from the omnipresent restrictions of the newly secure perimeter.

Lush, rolling greenery has replaced packed dirt, concrete, and asphalt

In Chinese, two brush strokes symbolize the word "crisis." One means danger, the other opportunity.

Danger and opportunity. Wind and iron. Brutal attacks and soft landscaping. Not all of these can abide by the hidden rules of harmony that Gustave Eiffel achieved. We do the best we can.

# RATS!

I am writing this in 2020, the Year of the Rat in the Chinese Zodiac. In fact, 2020 is the Year of the Gold Rat who is intelligent, witty, charming, ambitious, practical, alert, outgoing, and adaptable. The Gold Rat symbolizes creativity, honesty, and generosity. That's a lot to celebrate.

In Paris, as in all large cities, every year is the Year of the Rat, but no one celebrates that. I caught my first sight of a Parisian rat this year just before it scurried down a drain hole with its dinner of fast-food leftovers, leaving the Pret-a-Manger packaging behind.

No matter how cute Disney cartoons may make rodents, street rats are a problem. They are prolific. That alone is a problem, as a single pair of rats can establish a colony of over 15,000 descendants within one year.  They are destructive. That is a problem as they cause billions of dollars worth of damage, gnawing through lead, steel, concrete, and just about any sort of material. Rodents are voracious and destroy twenty percent of the world's crops in the fields. They spread disease and have caused more human deaths over the centuries than any other creature.

A colony of rats is called a mischief. That is an understatement.

In 2016, rat infestations had become such a problem in Paris that the city had to close a number of parks and squares. In January 2018, Paris launched a €1.7 million campaign against rats, including futile attempts at extermination with poisons. Anti-rat grids were installed under park landscaping to keep rats from surfacing.

The campaign also targeted humans. New rat-proof trash bins sprouted up in parks and squares and a poster campaign urged the public to do their part in reducing the city's rat population by properly disposing of trash.

"Leave your waste on the ground and rodents proliferate.
Please dispose of your rubbish in the nearest bin."

One city hall official said, "Our priority is to make it difficult to access food by discouraging Parisians and tourists from leaving food on the ground. It is a question of incivility which, settled, will make it possible to fight effectively against the presence of rats."

No city, using whatever means, has successfully overcome its rat problem. Poisons, traps, suffocation, and lethal injections have been miserable failures, while often harming humans and other animals. Releasing trained dogs, ferrets, and cats on rat colonies have failed to eradicate them. In 2010, Chicago even unleashed sixty coyotes onto the city streets in a desperate and doomed effort to control the problem.

    New style, rat-proof trash bins

Old style bins that are open dining invitations for rats

Rats are survivors. Their colonies thrive while cities get more and more desperate.

Paris being Paris, city hall can't mount any campaign without some protests. The anti-rat campaign was no different. The city's Stop the Rats posters competed with posters depicting adorable, cuddly rats with big brown, pleading eyes. "Paris must act for the animals." "A progressive city does not massacre its inhabitants." A well-organized group called Paris Animaux Zoopolis plastered these posters everywhere, promoting their philosophy of peaceful coexistence with animals.

The city government and Paris Animaux Zoopolis want essentially the same thing. They want rats to stop being a problem.

It's fair to say that rats have always been and always will be a problem for humans. But that doesn't stop innovative problem solving. In Flagstaff, Arizona, SenesTech, a tiny company run by Loretta Mayer and Cheryl Dyer, might have a tasty solution, or at least a partial solution.

SenesTech's mission is to improve "the health of our world by humanely managing animal populations through fertility control." Towards this end, they developed ContraPest, a pink milkshake-like concoction that uses a species-specific chemical to neutralize a male rat's sperm cells. Their product is so species-specific they have different formulas for common brown Norway rats, black roof rats and the common house mouse. The active ingredients metabolize in less than ten minutes and quickly break down into non-toxic elements when exposed to soil or water.

ContraPest has been successfully tested in Indonesian rice fields, on South Carolina pig farms and in the New York City subway. The rats practically cue up to ingest it. Birth rates plummeted by forty percent in several studies. Washington DC uses it as part of its integrated pest management program. A study of rat activity throughout the city concluded that ContraPest contributed significantly to a 90% reduction in rat activity.

A couple of civic-minded, caring women in the Arizona desert developed a humane, non-toxic, affordable, easily administered, and effective means of reducing and perhaps even, dare we hope?, containing rat infestations. That is something everyone can celebrate.

April 4th is World Rat Day. Let's do our bit by properly disposing of our trash. And maybe celebrate the intelligence, adaptability, and creativity of rats and humans with a pink strawberry milkshake?

"Paris must act for animals."

UNE VILLE PROGRESSISTE
NE MASSACRE PAS SES HABITANT-ES

UNE VILLE PROGRESSISTE
NE MASSACRE PAS SES HABITANT-ES

#ParisAnimaux2020
PARIS DOIT AGIR POUR LES ANIMAUX.
NOUS VOULONS UNE VILLE EXEMPLAIRE EN MATIÈRE DE CONDITION ANIMALE.
ZOOPOLIS.FR

#ParisAnimaux2020
PARIS DOIT AGIR POUR LES ANIMAUX.
NOUS VOULONS UNE VILLE EXEMPLAIRE EN MATIÈRE DE CONDITION ANIMALE.
ZOOPOLIS.FR

#ParisAnimaux2020
PARIS DOIT AGIR POUR LES ANIMAUX.
NOUS VOULONS UNE VILLE EXEMPLAIRE EN MATIÈRE DE CONDITION ANIMALE.
ZOOPOLIS.FR

#ParisAnimaux2020
UNE VILLE PROGRESSISTE
NE MASSACRE PAS SES HABITANT-ES

#ParisAnimaux2020
UNE VILLE PROGRESSISTE
NE MASSACRE PAS SES HABITANT-ES

#ParisAnimaux2020

PARIS DOIT AGIR POUR LES ANIMAUX.
NOUS VOULONS UNE VILLE EXEMPLAIRE EN MATIÈRE DE CONDITION ANIMALE.
ZOOPOLIS.FR

#ParisAnimaux2020
PARIS DOIT AGIR POUR LES ANIMAUX.
NOUS VOULONS UNE VILLE EXEMPLAIRE EN MATIÈRE DE CONDITION ANIMALE.
ZOOPOLIS.FR

#ParisAnimaux2020
PARIS DOIT AGIR POUR LES ANIMAUX.
NOUS VOULONS UNE VILLE EXEMPLAIRE EN MATIÈRE DE CONDITION ANIMALE.
ZOOPOLIS.FR

# Fun with French

The freewheeling English language has over 600,000 words and counting. The most authoritative compilation of English words is the Oxford English Dictionary (OED). It began in 1857 when the London Philological Society formed an Unregistered Words Committee. The effort morphed into a call for the general public to submit words and their definitions for entry into a new comprehensive dictionary. Today this is called "crowdsourcing" and, yes, "crowdsourcing" is an entry in the current OED. From its inception, the OED has been a popularity poll for words used by any and all English speakers. New words are added every three months.

The more austere French language has about 70,000 words that are carefully selected and defended by l'Académie Française. The Académie was formed in 1635 when Cardinal Richelieu had Louis XIII sign an edict for its creation. For almost 400 years, this august institute of forty members, called Immortals, has strived to maintain the purity and eloquence of the French language.

Maurice Druon, a former head of the Académie, observed, "The language of a people is its soul." And it is highly political. Just as Charles de Gaulle questioned, "How can anyone govern a nation that has 246 types of cheese?" Louis XIII's court faced the difficulty of governing an expanding territory with multiple languages and cultures. As late as 2008, this continued to be an issue. The Académie opposed the French Government's proposal to constitutionally offer recognition and protection to regional languages spoken within France, including Flemish, Alsatian, Basque, Breton, Catalan, Corsican, Occitan, Gascon, and Arpitan.

The Académie has also maintained the dominance of the masculine form of nouns. It issued a simple, uncompromising "Non" against attempts to introduce feminine equivalents of traditionally masculine nouns. According to the Académie, a female government minister is "le ministre," not "la ministre." But, simple edicts can't always keep social change at bay. Because the Académie has no legal authority, "la ministre" continues to be used and the conflict is unresolved.

The Académie's reputation as elitist and sexist remains intact. In 2017, seventy-seven linguists published an editorial lambasting the Académie's "incompetence and anachronism." More prosaically, the journalist François Busnel described the Académie as "a fat, blind, suicidal whale stubbornly determined to beach itself on a rocky coast with everyone watching."

As the arbiter of the French language, the Académie is tasked with writing the official French dictionary. The first edition was published in 1694, nearly sixty years after the Académie was founded. It is a Sisyphean task. As soon as one edition is finished, the next one is begun.

Work on the ninth edition of the *Dictionnaire de l'Académie française*, began in 1986 and, as of May 2024, it is complete through the word "syzygy." There are no quarterly updates.

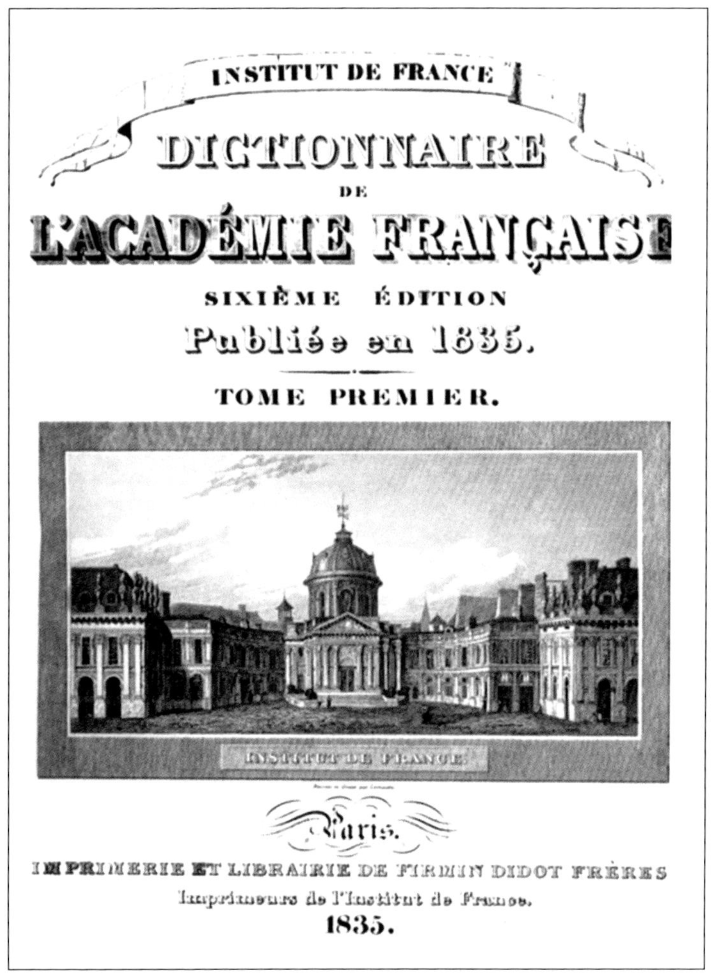


The title page of the 6th edition of the *Dictionary of the Académie*, showing the building housing the Institut de France, which is comprised of five Académies, including L'Académie Française.

Today, some argue, the Académie is less about unifying the French than about defending French against the incursion of English, which has come to dominate diplomatic and economic exchanges. Acceptance of English loanwords is a particularly difficult issue. The Académie has suggested variations of French words such as ordinateur, logiciel, and courriel be used instead of the English computer, software, and e-mail. "E-sports" should be "jeu video de competition." No French substitute was suggested for bitcoin or captcha, however, and they are now officially part of the French language.

The French are passionate about their language, and it is, undoubtedly, one of the most beautiful spoken languages in the world. That is certainly worth fighting to preserve. Part of the attraction for me of being in Paris is being surrounded by French speakers.

As a native English speaker whose attempts to learn any other language have been laughable at best, my relationship with French is flirtatious, superficial in its engagement, but appreciative of what I can't fully comprehend.

Examples of the fun I could have with French, in part because of my ignorance, were everywhere in my apartment. The button to start the microwave was labeled Depart. After a moment's thought, that was obvious. To depart is to start. The manual for the coffee pot explained in its literal translation into English, "This unit is equipped with an electrical outlet with earth and must earthed in an according plug." Again, this makes sense. Of course, energy and the earth are connected. It's just not usually explained so clearly.

During the transportation gréve (strikes, which are indeed related to grievances), my map app helpfully warned about le trafic perturbé. I was delighted. Perturbed traffic is not nearly as annoying as disrupted traffic. One can empathize with being perturbed. I pictured métro trains pursing their lips and shaking their heads petulantly at their troubles.

Sometimes getting along in Paris without knowing French seems impossible but I never feel at a loss when I'm there. Almost universally, the people are kind and understanding. Despite the Académie's staid sexism, French is fun.

Fun idioms:

- Peigner la giraffe / To comb the giraffe / To engage in a long, pointless task

- Il ne casse pas trois pattes à un canard / It doesn't break three legs on a duck / It's nothing special

- Manger sur le pouce / To eat on the thumb / To grab a quick bite

- Entre chien et loup / Between dog and wolf / Twilight

- Noyer le poisson / To drown the fish / To avoid the issue

- Avoir le cafard / To have the cockroach / To be depressed

- Ce n'est pas la mer à boire / It's not the sea to drink / It's not too much to ask

- L'ésprit d'escalier / stairway wit / to think of a witty response after you've left

- Chanter en yaouter / to sing in yogurt / to sing a song you don't know

- Avoir l'air d'une poule qui a trouvé un couteau / To look like a hen that has found a knife / To be puzzled

- Un coup d'épée dans l'eau / A sword blow to the water / To waste one's time

# A Tale of Two Cities

Unlike Dickens, both cities in this case are Paris. Of course, any city has many cities within, but the past two weeks have given me contrasting experiences of Paris, both centered on the Louvre.

## The Louvre, Hotbed of Rebellion

I went to the Louvre on Friday, January 17th, to get an annual pass from Les Amis du Louvre. The Louvre is a ramblin' kind of museum. The main entrance is under I. M. Pei's Pyramid, but it also has two hidden entrances.

Both are off rue Rivoli in arched passages among multiple other entrances to places unknown. I had to duck in and out of several before finding what I thought was the correct one. Not being too sure, though, I hung around to suss out what other people were doing. Everyone seemed as confused as me, which is unusual.

Not knowing what else to do, I walked toward a roped area that led to one of the escalators with a security guard seated next to it. An imposing fellow stepped smack in front of me saying something quite firmly in a lot of French I didn't understand except for "L'museé est firme." The museum is closed.

Main entrance to the Louvre

I wasn't going to argue but, well, I didn't think so. Maybe I had to go to a different entrance. By the time I walked back around rue Rivoli to the Pyramid entrance, I saw a crowd of people. Damn it. Just what I was hoping to avoid with my oh-so-clever-Paris-insider hidden entrance.

But it wasn't the usual crowd. It was a crowd of boisterous demonstrators blocking the entrance and another crowd watching the demonstration. A number of people were heckling the demonstrators. Journalists were reporting live on the situation.

Officially closed or not, no one was getting into the Louvre. People were officially unhappy on all sides. I walked away into the drizzly, gray streets.

**The Louvre, Haven of Civility and Fine Art**

On January 23rd, I returned to the Louvre through the Pyramid entrance. With helpful directions from several people, I found the Amis du Louvre office discreetly tucked away in the loud, echoing center court. The office was sanctuary of calm. Two people were ahead of me in line. I eavesdropped intently on their conversation in French, hoping to understand anything useful for my transaction.

I learned that they could take my ID photo at the desk, and I would not have to go back past security to a photo kiosk. That was useful. I learned that the woman who was staffing the desk spoke some but not a lot of English. That was also useful and not too concerning since my request was simple. I learned that all of the literature was in French. Again, useful, though a little concerning because forms easily confusticate me. Then it was my turn.

In my practiced but halting, butchered French, I said, "Bonjour, Madame. Je voudrais achete un, une . . . um. . . Pass Annuel?" ("Hello. I would like to buy an . . . um . . . Annual Pass?") Practice did not make perfect but the woman, I'll call her Marie, smiled and understood.

Marie then spoke to me in rapid fire French for about thirty long seconds. I heard Leonardo. Knowing they had a special exhibition of Leonardo's work, I guessed from her disappointed demeanor that she was telling me the annual pass would not allow me into the Leonardo exhibit. I somehow conveyed that this was okay since I had a separate ticket for that.

She handed me the registration form and we engaged in some polite banter with a workable mix of French and English as she helped me fill it in. Was I in Paris long? Had I been to the Louvre before? I commented on how good her English was and apologized for my French. She shook her head and said, "Non! Non! We French like to hear the English, I mean the American, accent." I held onto that comforting thought for the remainder of my stay.

The coupe de grâce of this happy interaction was when she asked if I had a bag as she handed me the oversize *Grand Galerie, Le Journal du Louvre* magazine. With the security check firmly in mind, I said I had my purse.

[Tourist Tip: In the security line, purses and bags go on the conveyor. Do not empty your pockets. Open your coat but do not take it off. Don't wait to be called through the scanner, just keep the line moving. As an aside, a young woman tried to bring long scissors into the museum and was surprised she could not take it into the exhibits. Seriously? The security guard looked understandably disgusted. Anyway, back to Marie.]

Marie tilted her head, looked at my small purse and said, "Ah! I will get you one." She went around the corner and returned with a bag bearing the Amis du Louvre logo. "Oh! Merci, madame. Vous est trés gentille." ("Oh! Thank you, ma'am. You are very kind.")

She leaned in and confided in English, "Because no one is looking." I put my magazine into the bag and the bag over my shoulder. She looked pleased, stood tall, and said, "You will be our ambassador." I stood tall too. Appointed to be a Louvre Ambassador! I walked away proud and exuberant into a palace of some of the finest art on earth.

# The Labyrinth of the Louvre

Disclaimer: What you are about to read reflects only the experience of the author who is admittedly and irrevocably directionally challenged. Hundreds and hundreds of thousands of people navigate the Louvre all the time without any issues.


Lord have mercy. Getting around the Louvre. Don't get me started.

But I did start.

In its defense, it must be stated up front that the Louvre is the largest art museum in the world. It exhibits approximately 38,000 objects dating from prehistory to the 21st century. It stores an addition 422,000 pieces. The exhibits cover more than an acre and a half of floor space in over 300 rooms on four floors in different buildings that have been cobbled together over the last three and a half centuries.

Complications began immediately. There are three entrances. The main entrance, where you see the long lines outside, is through the Pyramid. The second, less dramatic entrance, with much shorter lines, is accessed through the underground shopping mall, the Carrousel du Louvre. This entrance is marked by red banners off rue Rivoli. The third entrance, at the Porte des Lions, near the western end of the Denon wing, also accessed off of rue Rivoli but without any banners. This entrance is reserved for museum staff, certain guided groups, and annual pass holders.

You pass through security at all entrances and must descend an escalator. Everyone ends up in the grand, cacophonous, underground foyer, the Hall of Napoléon.

Three escalators ring the hall, each leading back up to different wings of the museum, the Denon, Richelieu or Sully, where the exhibits are located. Along the walls of the Hall of Napoléon are several information desks stocked with large, fold-out maps in numerous languages. Helpful, multilingual staff are usually behind the counter to answer questions. The hall also has a locker room to store personal items, though the one time I squeezed in I had no luck finding an empty locker. A bank of kiosks to buy individual entry tickets are in a room just off the hall.

Each of the three wings has four floors. Scattered between the floors are mezzanines. Hither and thither and yon various courtyards are sprinkled about. You know. Just for fun. There is also a map of closed sections for different days of the week. I didn't find out about that until my third visit. So, yeah. There's that too.

The three wings are supposed to be connected somehow without having to backtrack. I think. Can't be sure. I always had to exit the wing I was in, descend the elevator back to the Hall of Napoléon, wait in another line, and ascend another escalator to the different wing.

It's not that the maps are bad. It's that there's too much information. A 3-D map to clarify connections between the floors, mezzanines and courtyards could be helpful but it would hardly be practical and maybe even more confusing.

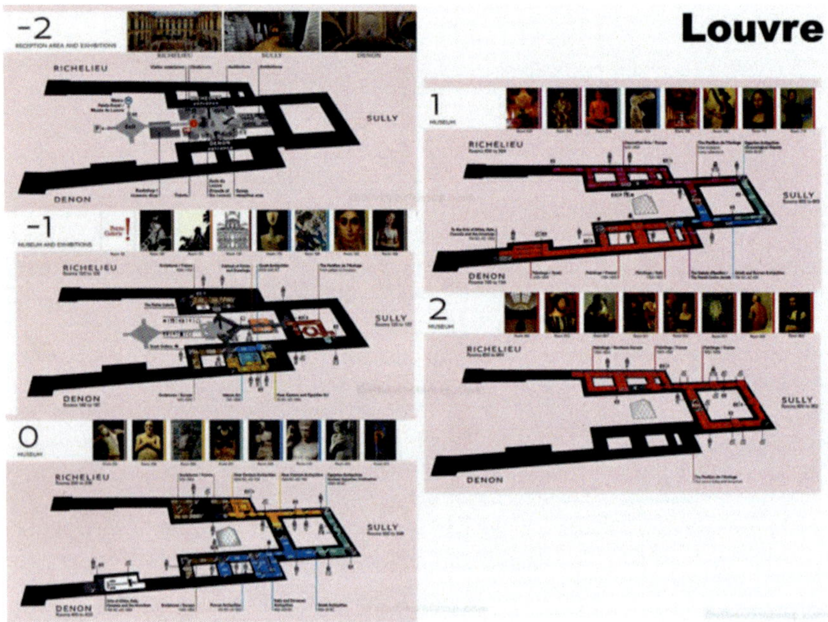

The stairwells are where it really gets interesting. Here, we enter the realm of Escher. Or Hogwarts with its moving staircases. Or the Minotaur's labyrinth. If it had stairs.

Somewhere in some wing of the Louvre

Did I mention the temporary passage that sometimes appeared out of nowhere? A secret passage that linked different wings. I happened upon it twice in my dozen visits and was glad when I did as it had some of the most helpful signage anywhere in the museum. There may have been more than one. Hard to tell.

As far as signage, I have to give a shout out to the ubiquitous and playful Mona Lisa signs. Even if you aren't headed to the Mona Lisa, these signs are extremely useful for orienting oneself.

Finally, there is a disconnect between how an artwork's location is listed in guidebooks and how the maps are labeled. Knowing a work of art is in X Gallery or Salon isn't helpful when the map doesn't show any X Gallery or Salon. The rooms just have numbers. That was fun.

The confusion is compounded by the crowds. Holding a large open map, looking around for a room number or sign and not crashing into any of the 15,000 people who visit the Louvre each day is a feat of no small skill.

The Salle Daru, not to be confused with the Galerie Daru, which is one floor below

All this being said, there are definitely ways to cope with the labyrinthine buildings and overwhelming crowds.

As for the crowds, if you have the option, go on a Wednesday or Friday evening when most of the tour groups have gone. You will also get some stunning views of the space after dark.

If you can't go during off-peak hours, take deep breaths, and think Zen thoughts. It might also help to treat the crowds as part of the exhibitions.

One of the sweetest moments of my time in the Louvre was sitting in front of Jacques-Louis David's monumental painting *Le Sacre de Napoléon*. I was enjoying the painting, but I enjoyed even more watching a vignette in front of the painting.

An elderly man was talking to a young girl, no more than five, as an elderly woman sat beside them. He pointed to the painting and the little girl would follow along attentively as he talked. I was enchanted by her concentration, expecting her to get restless at any moment as the pointing and talking went on for a good fifteen minutes.

All the while, people jockeyed in front of them for a good position to have their photo taken. They hardly glanced at Napoléon crowning himself. People weren't being pushy and, in fact, were being quite polite, but there was still a sense of frenzy around the painting.

Eventually, the elderly man took the little girl by the hand, and they walked over for a closer look. With a little coaxing, the little girl stood near – but not in front of – the painting to have her photo taken. I don't know what will happen to that photo, but the image of her standing there so respectfully will stay with me forever.

As for getting around, my best advice is to study the maps and room closures. Know as many ways as you can to identify the location of artwork. Allow extra time to see what you want and be open to surprise treasures discovered on an unexpected detour.

Maybe also have a glass of wine or two before plunging into the wildly unpredictable labyrinthine wonderland of the Louvre.

## Mona Lisa

So much – some say too much – has been made of Mona Lisa a/k/a La Joconde (French), La Gioconda (Italian).

She has been mobbed by admirers and even kidnapped. She now resides behind bullet proof glass with several ever-vigilant guards flanking her. She has been trivialized in endless variations of souvenirs. She has been relentlessly mocked. Though hundreds of thousands flock to see her every year, few look at her. Rather, they look to see themselves posed in front of her. There have been endless speculations and at least one suicide over her smile.

The crowd's view of *Mona Lisa*

I have my own theory about her smile. I think she is smiling across the room at another painting, *The Wedding Feast at Cana* by Veronese. It is the largest painting in the Louvre, in striking contrast to Mona Lisa's petite portrait. It is colorfully overstuffed with people at a raucous party in contrast to Mona Lisa's solitary composure. In perhaps the most glaring contrast, it is largely ignored.

Mona Lisa's view of the crowd with Veronese's *The Wedding Feast at Cana* in the background

I think within those contrasts there is a connection. I think Mona Lisa is having a private tête-à-tête with a woman at the wedding feast who is tilting her head, looking back at Mona Lisa, perhaps bored with the party.

I wonder what they are saying to one another.

Detail of *The Wedding Feast at Cana*

# Winged Victory of Samothrace

She stands triumphant on the bow of her ship, meeting the wind head-on, victorious.

Victorious… and a version of Frankenstein's monster.

The statue, or rather its pieces, were unearthed on the Greek island of Samothrace in 1863 by Charles Champoiseau, a French diplomat and amateur archeologist. The pieces of the ship were found a couple of decades later by an Austrian archeological team.

She stands so solidly strong, with her gossamer dress so delicately clinging to her torso that it is hard to see how fragmented she is.

It was only as I walked around toward her back that I saw the heavy metal supports on her wings. My immediate thought was, "Good for her." Anyone standing alone against such a gale should have some support.

The statue, dating back to 190 BCE, had been carved from several blocks. The head and upper torso were carved from one block, the lower torso was another. The arms, wings, feet, and part of the drapery were added from other blocks. After the Louvre acquired her in 1884, she had to be stitched back together.

The left wing was reconstructed from original fragments found on the site and has to be supported by a metal frame. Only a few fragments of the right wing had been found, so it was completely reconstructed as a plaster cast in a mirror image of the left wing. Her left torso and belt, also missing, were reconstructed in plaster in order to attach her left wing. Her head and arms are, obviously, completely missing.

The odd thing is, she feels complete.

She is fragmented, recast, braced, beheaded, and amputated. And yet . . . she is whole and wholly inspiring. She stands tall and beautiful and delicate and strong. She stands victorious.

## Love Locks

As I walked along the Seine in 2010, I saw a strange glimmer in the distance. As I walked closer, I came to a bridge with sparkling railings. The sparkles turned out to be padlocks. How curious.

The padlocks were symbolic "love locks." The bridge was the Pont des Arts, which crosses the Seine just downstream from the Île de la Cité. Apparently, starting in late 2008, in the mysterious way that fads begin, couples marked padlocks with their names or initials and attached them to the railings. Then, they would toss the key into the Seine, thereby declaring their undying commitment to be forever bound in love.

The romantic gesture became more and more popular. When there was no more room on the grates of the railings, locks were attached to other locks in insistent cascades of romance.

Eventually, the locks became a menace. Over six feet of the Pont des Arts bridge fell into the Seine in 2014 because of the weight of the locks. With little success, the city began a campaign, Love Without Locks, suggesting other ways for lovers to channel their declarations of love. By 2015, there were over one million locks on the Pont des Arts, weighing over forty-five tons. Paris, the City of Love, didn't want to break anyone's heart, but the locks had to go.

To ease the heartache of the locks' removal, the city announced in December 2016 that some of the locks would be auctioned off and the rest sold as scrap metal. All of the proceeds would be distributed to charities. As expressed by Bruno Julliard, First Deputy Mayor of Paris at the time, this was "to symbolically pursue the message of affection and love that couples from all over the world wanted to share when they came to Paris and installed these locks."

Only three percent of the locks could be auctioned off. The rest were so toxic, they were not even fit for use as scrap metal.

The railings' grates were replaced with clear plexiglass. You can't put a lock on it, so tourists graffiti it with with amorous messages. One entrepreneurial woman was still selling heart shaped locks on the bridge when I walked by in 2020. Stubbornly determined lovers were still locking up the lampposts.

The lovelock habit defiantly spread to anything that a lock could be attached to. Combination locks joined the keyed locks. This last innovation strikes me as being at odds with the original intent. Proactively jot down a few numbers and you can return anytime to retrieve the lock. Certainly, this a more contingent, though perhaps a more realistic, sort of commitment?

I haven't been the only one questioning the meaning of all of these expressions of love.

A temporary art installation next to the Louvre, titled *Chez Nous* (*Our House*), used the locks themselves as a critique. The artist, Carmel Mariscal, welded panels of love-locked grating from the Ponts des Arts bridge into the shape of a building. According to the project curator, "*Chez Nous* questions the tradition of locking love." The construction is fragile, and passersby are instructed not to touch it.

In the ironic way life has of unveiling our foibles, the love locks provide an uncomfortably accurate metaphor about the true nature of love. If you try to lock it up, love will only deteriorate with time and become worthless, at best a temporary work of art that must not be touched.

Paris has a lot to teach about love.

Chez Nous sculpture

Worthless expressions of undying love

# Joy

Outside Les Halles

# Philippe

It simply would not do to have been in Paris for almost three months and not to have fallen in love.

This past week, a gentleman has been out on his balcony just across the street from my window, tending his garden and joining in the evening applause for the health care workers.

I have named him Philippe. I have also decided he is intelligent and kind, curious and passionate. He is well read without pretensions and has a generous spirit with a delightful sense of humor. He revels in café conversations. He is not afraid of philosophy or whimsy. He plays the oboe. And, as you can see, he's not bad looking.

My trip is now complete.

# J'existe.

C'est tout.
C'est suffit.

That's all.
It's enough.

# PART IV

## COVID-19

---

January 1, 2020

to

December 31, 2020

# COVID-19

# COVID-19 Timeline

This was planned as the trip of a lifetime. Little did I know.

At times it seemed that Paris was truly under siege during my three-month stay. It had suffered crippling, record-breaking strikes and protests. The Seine flooded. Windstorms raged. Then came a plague in the form of the novel coronavirus.

It's hard to remember now the slow evolution of our understanding of the nature of the virus, its potential to spread, best treatment practices and the debates about elimination versus containment versus herd immunity.

What I will always remember is the kindness, patience, understanding and support of family and friends.

Note: The statistics in this timeline are only an indication of trends. Because of wide variations and discrepancies in testing and reporting, they were recognized, even at the time, as rough approximations.

*Thursday, January 1*
The Huanan Seafood Wholesale Market is shut down for cleaning.

*Thursday, January 9*
The World Health Organization (WHO) announces the existence of a mysterious coronavirus-related pneumonia in Wuhan, China.

*Saturday, January 11*
China records its first death linked to the virus.

*Thursday, January 16*
I arrive in Paris by Eurostar from London. The news is dominated by the massive strikes and demonstrations that have disrupted almost every aspect of French life since December 5, 2019, closing down the métro and many cultural institutions, including the Eiffel Tower.

*Monday, January 20*
The Centers for Disease Control (CDC) says the US will begin screening for coronavirus at JFK, San Francisco International, and LAX airports.

*Tuesday, January 21*
The first US case is confirmed in Washington state. Scientists in China confirm human-to-human transmission of the virus.

*Wednesday, January 23*
China places Wuhan's population of over 11 million people under quarantine. All events for the Lunar New Year, starting on January 25th, are cancelled.

*Friday, January 24*
I hunker down in the apartment after seeing vans of police in riot gear congregate on the Place Joachim-du-Bellay and move out toward Blvd de Sébastopol where tens of thousands will be marching to protest proposed pension reforms.

*Wednesday, January 29*
I get my hair cut by Céline at Olive Hair Line, 3 Rue des Prouvaires, a couple of blocks away from my apartment.

*Thursday, January 30*
WHO declares the virus a Public Health Emergency of International Concern.

*Friday, January 31 to Saturday, February 1*
I have a high fever and pass out on the kitchen floor in the middle of the night while getting myself something to drink. I crawl back to bed.

*Sunday, February 2*
The fever breaks and I rest in bed. The first coronavirus death outside China is recorded in the Philippines.

*Tuesday, February 4*
The Diamond Princess cruise ship is quarantined in Yokohama harbor for a fourteen-day observation period after a passenger who had disembarked died of "Covid pneumonia."

*Thursday, February 6*
The first known US death from the virus is recorded in California.

*Sunday, February 9*
I make train and hotel reservations for a Paris-Milan-Marseilles trip from March 24 – 27.

A second wave of locusts, which have been invading East Africa since late 2019, begins swarming as the primary growing season starts. In Kenya, one swarm, covering 930 square miles, is the largest on record. Famine is expected to be widespread.

*Tuesday, February 11*
I file my federal and state income taxes online. WHO announces the disease caused by the novel coronavirus will be called Covid-19.

*Friday, February 14*
I buy a ticket to see *Edmond* at the Palais Royal Theatre. I also buy a train ticket for a day trip to Zurich.

A tourist from China tests positive for the virus and dies in France. This is Europe's first death due to the virus.

*Saturday, February 15*

The US arranges charter planes to evacuate citizens off the Diamond Princess.

*Sunday, February 16*

I meet up with my friend Pat and her friend who arrive in Paris for a week. I turn sixty-two.

*Tuesday, February 18*

The Diamond Princess reports 542 confirmed cases.

*Wednesday, February 19*

Passengers who are confirmed free from the virus begin to disembark from the Diamond Princess.

*Wednesday, February 26*

Two more deaths due to the novel coronavirus are announced in Paris.

I continue to visit the Louvre and Café de Flore.

As insurance for an alternative to a return voyage on the QM2, I book a nonstop Paris-to-Denver flight on Norwegian Air for $368, including two checked bags with an exit row aisle seat and priority boarding. It departs April 15th.

*Thursday, February 27*

Extreme winds with gusts up to 70 mph hit Paris.

*Saturday, February 29*

Hand sanitizer disappears from the shelves at Monoprix. The television news starts to broadcast government alerts about the virus.

*Le Monde* publishes articles about: how to wash one's hands; a deadly attack at Gare Lyon; horse racing results; a review of the Louboutin exhibit; and the windstorm's destructive aftermath.

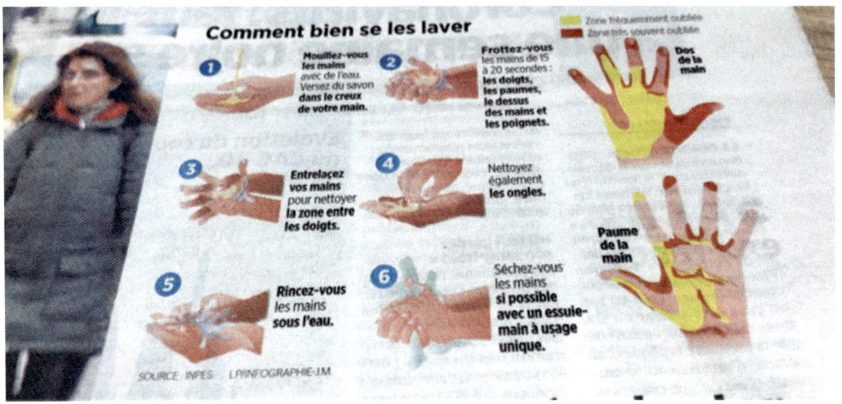


*Sunday, March 1*
Theatres are open. I attend the matinee performance of *Edmond*.

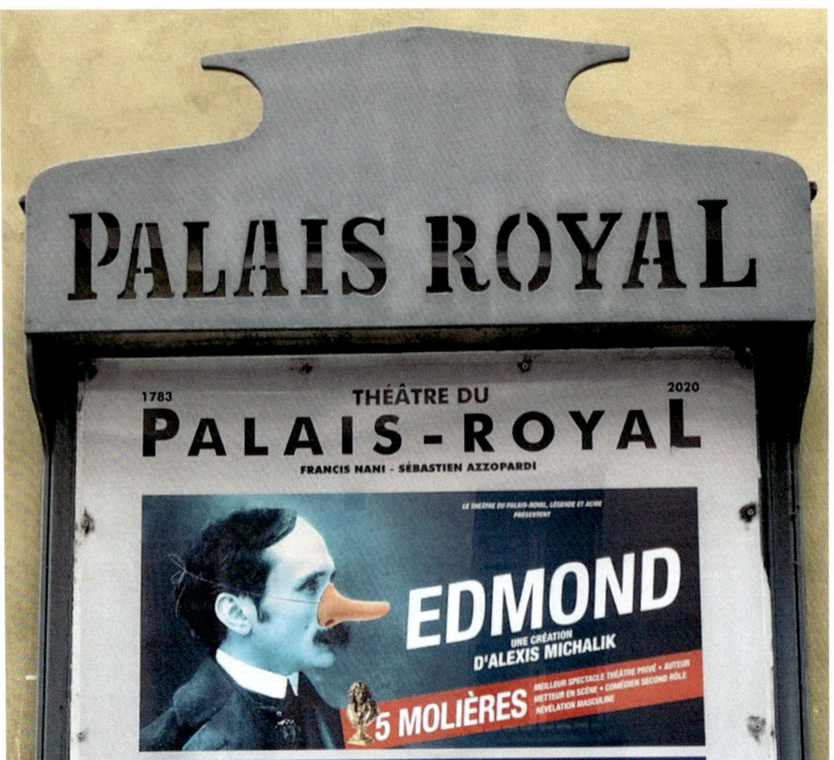

The Louvre closes due to staff concerns about the spread of the virus.

My friends, Gina and Lynn, discuss their impending travel to Paris from New Mexico. Because of family concerns, Gina decides to stay home. Lynn decides to come to Paris.

I start getting a sore throat and nasal congestion. I have no cough or fever.

> France: 103 cases; 3 deaths.
> Italy: 1,694 cases; 34 deaths.

*Monday, March 2*
Lynn arrives in Paris. Despite my now fully fledged head cold, I'm hopeful about going on the Canal St. Martin boat trip that we had booked and to the Louboutin exhibit for which we have tickets.

Ireland cancels Dublin's St. Patrick's Day Parade.

*Wednesday, March 4*
I'm laid up with my cold. Lynn makes toast and tea for a breakfast-in-bed for me and goes shopping for chicken soup ingredients. The Canal St. Martin boat trip is cancelled because the Seine is flooded.

*Thursday, March 5*
Lynn goes to the Louboutin exhibit alone.

*Friday, March 6*
I contact the Glam Hotel in Milan to cancel my reservation for the night of March 24 - 25 due to the spread of the virus in northern Italy. They write back saying the problem is in the Lodi area where containment is already under way and that Milan has taken preventative measures that they hope will keep the virus away. They ask me not to cancel the reservation pending further developments. I keep the reservation. (They send a full refund in October without my asking.)

I book a train ticket from Paris to Marseilles, assuming the Milan portion of the trip will have to be cancelled, but still hoping I can get to Marseilles for a couple of nights.

Lynn's good cooking has cured my cold enough for us to get out and about a bit.

*Saturday, March 7*
United Airlines emails about their response to the coronavirus outbreak, offering free changes for flights booked from March 7 to 31.

France: 949 cases; 16 deaths.
Italy: 5,883 cases; 233 deaths.

*Sunday, March 8*
I hear from my sister Jeanne about shoppers stocking up on toilet paper at Costco in Naperville and about a Chicago school shutting down because a teacher's aide had contact with someone who had contact with someone who had the virus. Students are being sent home from some college campuses in the US.

I research the mathematics of contagion.

$R$ = reproduction #
i.e. how worried should we be?

If $R > 1$, each infected person will, on average, give it to at least one other person + the disease will grow.

Duration — how long someone is infectious
Opportunity — how many people the infected person comes into contact with
Transmission Probability — the odds of an infection getting across in a contact
Susceptibility — the chance the other person will become infected + infectious
(vaccines)

$R = D \times O \times T \times S$

Parks near the Seine close due to flooding.

Italy imposes a quarantine throughout its northern region of Lombardy, affecting over 16 million people.

Italy: 7,375 cases; 366 deaths.

*Monday, March 9*
Lynn and I take my nonfunctional MacBook Air to be repaired at Cyber-Jay, a small, independent Apple repair shop on the Left Bank.

The Louvre staff are "highly vigilant" as they monitor the Seine's flood level.

Italy goes into national lockdown, affecting 60 million people.

*Tuesday, March 10*
Lynn and I go to Le Train Bleu for lunch. Commercial advertisements at Gare de Lyon are being replaced with public service announcements about how to slow the spread of the virus.

I cancel my return on the QM2 on the last day to get a fifty percent refund. I also cancel my Amtrak reservations from New York to Denver.

*Wednesday, March 11*
The CDC issues guidelines advising against traveling on cruise ships.

WHO declares the outbreak a pandemic.

*Thursday, March 12, 2 a.m.*
(Wednesday evening, March 11, in the US)
Gina calls from New Mexico to tell us that the US president has ordered a complete travel ban from Europe for thirty days, beginning Friday the 13th.

Lynn is scheduled to leave later that morning. She gives me her extra sanitizing wipes, hand sanitizing gel, gloves, and an N95 mask.

I don't even try to get a flight out of Paris before the travel ban goes into effect and decide to sit tight for the time being. My April 15th departure on Norwegian Airlines is just after the thirty-day ban expires, assuming it isn't extended.

I make contingency plans in case I am not able to leave Paris on April 15th, exploring the possibility of extending the lease on the Paris apartment.

I check flights out of London. The US ban exempts flights from the UK and travel is still possible from Paris to London.

Lynn makes her flight that morning, bypassing the insanity of panicked travelers at Charles de Gaulle International Airport since she didn't check a bag. The news reports that some people have paid $20,000 for last minute return flights.

I go to the Louvre, which has reopened to limited capacity. I am able to get in with my Amis de Louvre pass.

The main entrance to the Louvre during lockdown restrictions

*Thursday, March 12, cont.*
My son Zach writes that the District of Columbia is under a state of emergency, and he expects to start working from home as soon as the federal government gets teleworking agreements in place for federal contractors.


*Friday, March 13*
My sister Joan writes to say that schools in Nashville, Tennessee, where her daughter teaches, are closing for the rest of the year. My mom had gone to Mass the previous Sunday, but Joan and she agreed she would stop going for the foreseeable future.

The trees around St. Eustache are in full bloom.

I go to Monoprix to stock up on food.

The US State Department clarifies the travel ban does not apply to returning US citizens.

European governments express displeasure that they were not informed or consulted about the US ban before it was publicly announced.

Photos are posted online of chaotic crowds crunched into corridors at O'Hare waiting to get through passport control and customs.

I go to Café de Flore and, on the way home, buy a cheap ASUS laptop since my laptop is still at the repair shop. With all the confusion and uncertainty, I don't want to be without this vital source of information and communication.

Lynn arrives safely in Santa Fe and begins her two weeks of self-isolation as required of people arriving in NM from hotspots.

Schools in France close. Parisians with country homes begin to leave the city. By March 20th, seventeen percent of Parisians will have left.

The US declares a national emergency.


*Saturday, March 14*
I'm closely monitoring the flight situation. Norwegian Air has cancelled about half of their flights to the US, but my flight is still listed as scheduled.

Family and friends relate stories of panic buying in the US.

News starts to filter in that US citizens returning from Europe "will be funneled through certain airports and processed." No word yet on which airports will do the funneling or what the "processing" will entail.

It is the 70th consecutive Saturday that the Gilets Jaunes have staged protests, closing most métro stations.

I take a walk to the Left Bank and stop in at Café de Flore. The entire second floor is empty. After two hours other people come in. I ask for l'addition (the bill). I make my way to Shakespeare and Company to stock up on books, anticipating a longer-than-planned stay in Paris. Along the way, I snap photos and say my good-byes to favorite sights.

I take the métro back to my apartment. The mood is solemn. Four young men start singing a rousing song familiar to the other passengers. Some passengers join in. The mood shifts to one of camaraderie in crisis.

I get off at the Les Halles stop and go to Monoprix to stock up on more items. Though the store is crowded, the shelves are full.

Toilet paper shelves in Monoprix

Cash payments are discouraged due to contagion concerns. I bring home a ten-inch raspberry tart and take stock of my "essentials" gathered that day.

Norwegian Airlines emails that they have cancelled my flight. I fill out the refund request.

I buy a ticket from United for a code-share flight on Air Canada for March 26th, arriving in Chicago via Montreal.

Jeanne and her husband Kurt, a pilot with United, offer to let me stay in their guest room in Naperville, Illinois, to self-quarantine for two weeks after I arrive in Chicago. Jeanne suggests the possibility of using one of Kurt's standby passes to fly to the US.

The Diocese of Joliet cancels all in person Sunday masses. Schools in the US are closing. Colleges move to online classes.

All non-essential businesses in France close as of midnight.

I spend the night listening to an audio of *Wind in the Willows*.

France: 3600 cases; 79 deaths.
Italy: 21,000  cases; 1,441 deaths.

*Sunday, March 15*
I count out my prescription medications. I have enough to get me through mid-July. I learn that the Paris lockdown is scheduled for thirty days.

I start reading *The Rules of Contagion: Why Things Spread - And Why They Stop* (2020).


*Sunday, March 16*
I learn online that computer repair shops, les vendeurs et réparateurs d' ordinateurs, are considered essential services.

Germany closes its borders except for transporting goods and workers.

Louis Vuitton retools its perfume manufacturing to make hand sanitizer to donate to the 39 hospitals in Paris.

A local homeless person, the Lady with the Green Tent, is gone.

Most of Europe is under some form of lockdown.

The news lists what is deemed essential in different countries:

France – wine and tobacco shops, bakeries, and computer repair shops
Belgium – hair salons, friteries stands, and bookstores
Austria – parks and playgrounds
Poland – Catholic masses
The Netherlands – coffee shops and cannabis dispensaries

I research the "burden of illness" between the usual flu season and the novel coronavirus. The most recent data available from the CDC is from the 2018-2019 season:

35.5 million are sick
16.5 million visit a doctor
500,000 are hospitalized
34,500 die
1 per 1,000 fatality rate

US Covid-19 fatality rate as of mid-March is 18 per 1,000, 18 times higher than the "regular flu." Italy's fatality rate is 111 per 1,000. The high rate in Italy is explained in part by the fact that their population is disproportionately elderly and because most of their households are multi-generational.

Macron addresses the nation.

*Tuesday, March 17*
As of noon, anyone venturing outdoors in Paris is required to carry an Attestation form with identification information and the reason for being outside one's residence. A new form is required for each outing.

Notices of closures appear on shop windows.

I see a hand-written sign on blvd. Saint-Germain that I roughly translate as: "In accordance with the directives of the prime minister, your store Maison Georges Larnicol will remain closed until further notice. If you wish, you can find our products on our website: www.larnicol.com."

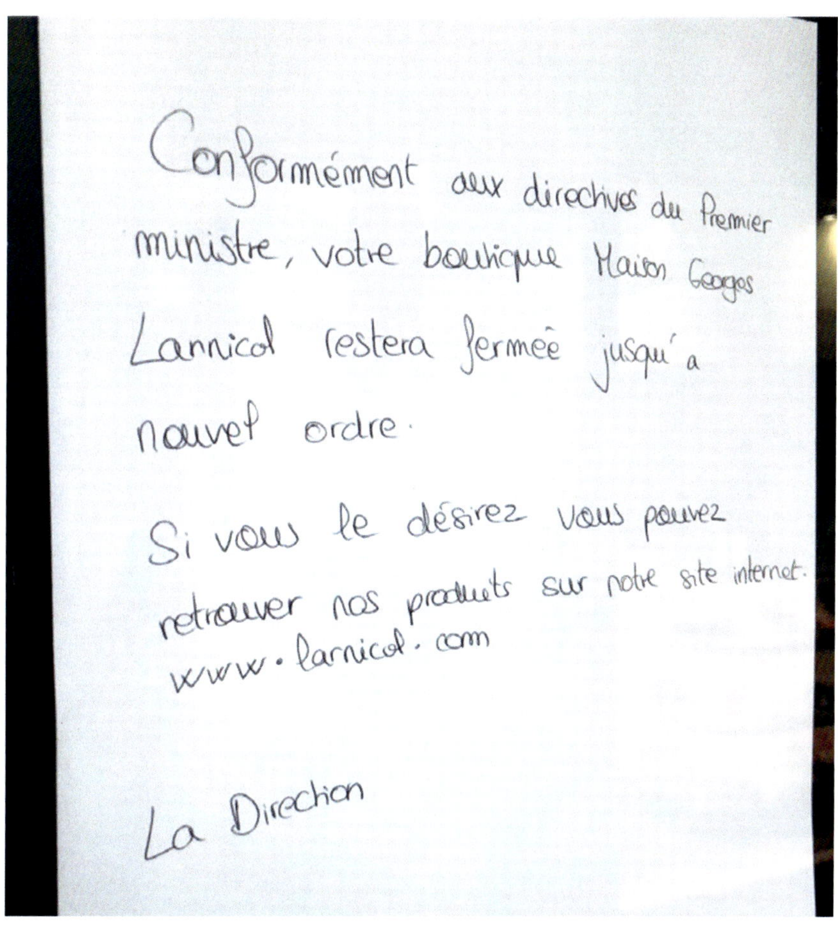


La Maison Georges Larnicol chocolate shop

I read another sign in a pizza shop window: "Following the coronavirus, we are forced to close our restaurant. While waiting, take care of yourself, be vigilant, and keep morale high! See you soon."

More advertising space is replaced with public notices on preventing the spread of the coronavirus.

I ration my food for the next fifteen days.

A local homeless person, the Man with Two Bags, is still around but has moved to the other side of the Fountain of the Innocents.

Not being sure when I will leave, I write down a daily routine for lockdown, including exercising by walking up and down the apartment stairs. I check out US television shows dubbed into French: NCIS, Columbo, Little House on the Prairie, Gossip Girl, and Big Bang Theory.

Residents in the neighborhood start to open their windows at 8 p.m. and clap in thanks to the health care workers. I join in.

The Eiffel Tower continues to shine its beam over the city.

Santa Fe County announces its first confirmed case.

France: 31,500 cases; 2,503 deaths.

*Wednesday, March 18*
Canada imposes entry restrictions:

**Effective March 18 at 12:01 ET**

All foreign nationals that have been outside the country in the last 14 days are prohibited from traveling to Canada.

For flights to Canada, only the following travelers are permitted to board:

- **Canadian and Canadian Permanent Residents**

- **Foreign nationals that are continuing into a third country (for example, a traveler from EUROPE via Canada and to the U.S.) are permitted to board.**

- **The traveler must meet other requirements such as the U.S. or other country entry restrictions.**

- **U.S. nationals departing the U.S. only and arriving in Canada will be permitted to board.**

*Thursday, March 19*
I check flights to the US from anywhere in Europe. They are getting scarce.

The streets are all but deserted. The métro is running very few trains.

I bring some cheese, bread, and juice to the Man with Two Bags who wears a white plastic rosary around his neck.

Officials in France predict that infections will peak in May as long as people adhere to the lockdown rules. I contemplate staying in Paris through June.

I fill out the Attestation form, checking the "exercise in close proximity to my home" box and take a brisk walk to celebrate the last day of winter.

## ATTESTATION DE DÉPLACEMENT DÉROGATOIRE

En application de l'article 1er du décret du 16 mars 2020 portant réglementation des déplacements dans le cadre de la lutte contre la propagation du virus Covid-19 :

Je soussigné(e)

(Mme)/ M.  *Carol Couch*

Né(e) le :  *16 Février 1958*

Demeurant :  *25 blvd de Sébastopol*
*75001*

certifie que mon déplacement est lié au motif suivant (cocher la case) autorisé par l'article 1er du décret du 16 mars 2020 portant réglementation des déplacements dans le cadre de la lutte contre la propagation du virus Covid-19 :

☐ déplacements entre le domicile et le lieu d'exercice de l'activité professionnelle, lorsqu'ils sont indispensables à l'exercice d'activités ne pouvant être organisées sous forme de télétravail (sur justificatif permanent) ou déplacements professionnels ne pouvant être différés;

☐ déplacements pour effectuer des achats de première nécessité dans des établissements autorisés (liste sur gouvernement.fr);

☐ déplacements pour motif de santé;

☐ déplacements pour motif familial impérieux, pour l'assistance aux personnes vulnérables ou la garde d'enfants;

☒ déplacements brefs, à proximité du domicile, liés à l'activité physique individuelle des personnes, à l'exclusion de toute pratique sportive collective, et aux besoins des animaux de compagnie.

Fait à *Couch Commune*, le *19* / *3* /2020

(signature)

Merci
Prenons soin
des soignants !
Soutenons-les.
JCDecaux

*Thursday, March 19, cont.*
I create and print out a "Do Not Resuscitate. Do Not Intubate." card to tape to my passport and put in my wallet.

Teams of Samu Sociaux de Paris, a charitable organization that provides emergency care to those who are sans domicile fixe, walk the streets, offering coffee, food, and other support.

*Friday, March 20*
I get an email from Cyber-Jay, but can't tell if my laptop is ready. My emails to them bounce back as undeliverable. No one is answering their phone.

Flights from Paris to the US become almost non-existent.

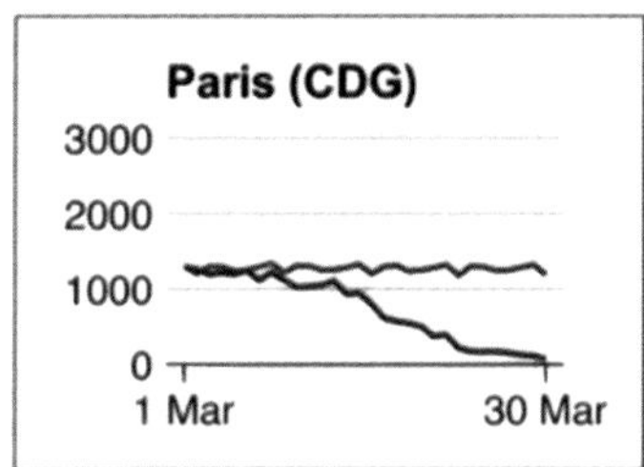


Source: Flightstats.com

The US Embassy in Paris sends out the following alert:

"If you are a US citizen who is staying in France, you should be prepared to remain abroad for an indefinite period and follow the Government of France's confinement orders."

Plagues of locusts continue to swarm in East Africa threatening hunger and starvation for millions in the region.

*Saturday, March 21*
I spend the afternoon working on refunds for the  train ticket to Zurich, the one-way tickets from my original Paris-Milan-Marseilles-Paris trip and the backup ticket from Paris to Marseilles.

I check on my Air Canada flight. Their website says they are not the operating carrier, and I should check with the operating carrier for further information. I go back to the United website. They say Air Canada is the operating carrier.

Illinois has issued a stay-at-home order. I call Jeanne. She assures me that she can still pick me up at O'Hare on the 26th.

My Duolingo lesson for the day . . . got that right.

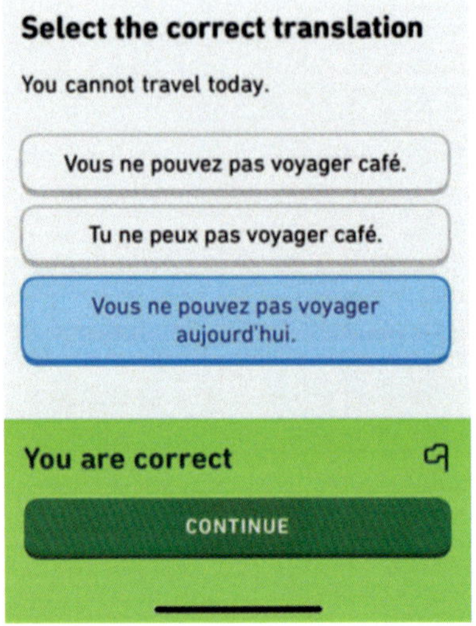


I purchase a backup ticket directly from Air Canada, reasoning I can cancel the ticket I bought through United and use the United credit for another flight at some later date. The backup ticket purchased directly through Air Canada's website can be cancelled within twenty-four hours at no cost.

I hear from Jeanne that United has added a flight that I might be able to get on using one of Kurt's standby passes.

The Man with Two Bags is gone.

> France: 14,459 cases; 562 deaths.
> Italy: 34,000 cases; 413 deaths.

Sunday, March 22
The possible standby United flight disappears.

Air Canada notifies me that the backup flight I purchased the previous day has been cancelled. It is within the 24 hour purchase window, so I cancel the ticket online to avoid having to request a refund or exchange.

The Diocese of Joliet starts live-streaming Sunday mass.

The QM2 officially cancels the Southampton to New York leg of their world cruise.

New York has become the worldwide epicenter of the outbreak with over 21,000 cases.

*Monday, March 23*
I walk over to Cyber-Jay on the Left Bank and find a note saying they are closed until March 30th. Anticipating this, I slip a prepared note through a gap in the door, asking them to ship my laptop back to New Mexico.

I risk taking a circuitous route home to see what the city is like under lockdown. The police stop me on rue Rivoli, close enough to the apartment, and are satisfied with my papers.

Streets are empty.

Rue Rivoli with the Louvre on the right

TABAC
RUFFNECK
Le Relais du Vin
Happy Hour
Les Halles
PITA KEBAB
BAOBAB
BAOBAB
VIANDE HALLAL
PLAT DU JOUR
KEBAB
Around my neighborhood

GIBERT JEUNE
GIBERT JEUNE
LLIAM Z
ENTREE
ENTREE
ENTREE

Place Joachim-du-Bellay pre-lockdown

Place Joachim-du-Bellay during lockdown

*Monday, March 23, cont.*
My flight on the 26th is listed as "on schedule." If the flight gets cancelled, I decide I would wait out the pandemic in Paris as there was the expectation that things would be more back to normal by summer. I look for cheaper apartment options online and strategize how to move apartments during the lockdown.

I began researching the best way to get to the airport. The RER may or may not be running. Taxis and Ubers aren't reliable. I contact Gina about the car service she has used for trips to and from the airport.

I debate about taking the apartment key with me in case I don't get on the flight and have to return to the apartment. If I do make it back to the US, I could mail the key back to the concierge.

I fill out two Attestation forms for the 26th. One for going to the airport and, just in case, one for getting back. I worry about my occasional, lingering cough from my head cold earlier in the month, knowing it wasn't Covid-19, but also knowing it could prevent me from boarding the plane.

New Mexico issues a statewide "stay-at-home" order, effective March 24th.

*Tuesday, March 24*
I get an email message from Cyber-Jay that my laptop is ready. I can pick it up at their second location on the Right Bank from 10 am to 1 pm Monday through Thursday. It's about 11 am. I reply, "Merci! Je vien tout suite!!!" ("Thank you! I'll come after it!!!", having meant to say, "I'm coming right away!!!") I get an email back, "Ok a tout de suite. Cordialement, Jeremy." ("Ok, see you later.")

I look up the shop address on the map. The shop is farther than the one-kilometer limit we are allowed to travel from our homes. I fill out another Attestation form, hoping not to be stopped. I dash out the door and soon get lost, of course, but reach the shop about an hour later.

A table blocks the entrance to the shop but Jeremy, standing behind the counter, smiles as I breathlessly explain who I am. He holds up the laptop to show me that it is working and tells me a bunch of stuff about the repair.

I put my credit card on the table at the door and step back into the street while he comes from around the counter to pick it up. With receipt, invoice, and laptop tucked in my bag and with many thanks to Jeremy, I head back home. I avoid the main thoroughfares and am not stopped by the police.

I book a ride with Citizen Limousine for early morning on the 26th.

The summer Olympics are postponed until 2021.

France: 20,149 cases; 860 deaths.
Italy: 63,927 cases; 6,077 deaths.
US: 46,450 cases; 524 deaths.

*Wednesday, March 25*
The Air Canada flight on the 26th continues to be listed as on time.

I pack my bags and arrange to give my leftover food to the concierge.

Hours later, Air Canada cancels the Montreal to Chicago flight for the 25th. I worry about what that means for my flights from Paris to Montreal to Chicago on the 26th. They are still listed as scheduled.

Still later, all reference to the Montreal to Chicago flight on the 26th disappears from Air Canada's website. The Paris to Montreal flight is still listed as on time. I start researching alternative flights from Montreal to Chicago, assuming I could still get to Montreal.

Still later yet, I am unable check in for either leg of my flights. I continue to plan to go the airport early the next morning allowing for plenty of extra time to find out in-person from Air Canada what is going on.

I take a video of the neighbors clapping at sunset.

*Thursday, March 26 – 1 a.m.*
Air Canada sends a notification that my Montreal to Chicago flight has been officially cancelled. Because I booked through United, Air Canada will not rebook me on an alternative flight.

Because of the ongoing uncertainty about Air Canada flights and because of the travel restrictions Canada has imposed, I decide to cancel all my flights and get a credit from United.

I stay awake the rest of the night so I can run downstairs in time to pay the driver from Citizen Limousine.

The concierge notices me walking back into the building and insists on bringing back the food I left for her. "Vous devez manger." ("You need to eat.")

A friend suggests I sign up for the US Embassy's "Smart Traveler" alerts. I do. I go back to bed.

The US, with over 82,000 confirmed cases, now leads the world in reported infections.

*Friday, March 27th*
I unpack.

In the window of La Maison Georges Larnicol
I have as much of a chance of catching a flight as this lapin does in making it to the moon.

As cases in the US skyrocket, I again plan to stay in Paris for the foreseeable future, working through my finances and budget.

> France: 28,786 cases; 1,695 deaths
> Italy: 80,539 cases; 8,165 deaths.
> US: 101,242; 1,588 deaths.

*Saturday, March 28*
France extends its lockdown to April 30th.

In the US, 6.6 million workers filed for unemployment benefits for the week ending March 28th, the highest number of initial claims ever filed.

*Sunday, March 29*
I celebrate European Daylight Savings Day by researching time zone trivia.

*Tuesday, March 31*
While shopping at Monoprix, I notice a pop-up resource desk for those experiencing domestic abuse.

Monoprix opens a small section for office supplies. I buy paper for the printer.

Thinking I will be in Paris for Easter on April 12th, I buy myself a herd of Lindt chocolate bunnies.

Over one-third of the world's population is in some form of lockdown.

> France: 56,989 cases; 4,032 deaths.
> Italy: 105,792 cases; 12,428 deaths.
> US: 189,753 cases; 4,745 deaths.

*Thursday, April 2*
I get a US Embassy alert that the Paris Prefecture of Police is allowing some extensions to stay for those who entered France through the ninety-day visa-free Schengen area travel policy and are unable to return to their country of origin due to the Covid-19 outbreak.

I research this online. There are still some commercial flights from Paris to the US and, unlike some countries that have completely shut their borders even to their own citizens, US citizens are still allowed to return. I do not qualify for the extension.

*Thursday, April 2, cont.*
I research the consequences of overstaying the ninety-day visa. One unlikely but possible scenario is that I will be banned from returning to the Schengen area, which includes most countries in Europe. My ninety days expires on April 15th. All hope of staying into the summer is dashed.

I search again for flights. Options are extremely limited. KLM has one flight a week that would get me to Chicago via Amsterdam. I book a fully refundable one-way flight for April 9th.

I call Citizen Limonsine again and schedule a car for the airport.

Worldwide: over 1,000,000 cases.

*Friday, April 3*
In France, 26,000 people are hospitalized nationwide with 6,000 in intensive care. Hospitals in the Paris region are reaching capacity and a special train is retrofitted as an intensive care unit to transport patients from Paris to eastern cities where more beds are available.

Rungis Market, just south of Paris, converts its refrigerated hall, separate from the rest of the market, into a temporary morgue as it had been in 2003 when a particularly brutal heat wave killed thousands of elderly people.

The US Embassy sends out the following message:

> International commercial flight options currently exist in France. US citizens who wish to return to the United States should make commercial arrangements as soon as possible unless they are prepared to remain abroad for an indefinite period. **The US government does not anticipate arranging repatriation flights from France at this time.** [emphasis in the original]

Australia tells tourists that it is time for them to go home.

France: over 60,000 cases; over 5,400 deaths.
Italy: over 85,000 cases; over 14,600 deaths.
US: 228,000 cases; over 5,300 deaths.

*Saturday, April 4*
I hand sew a face mask from a kitchen towel.

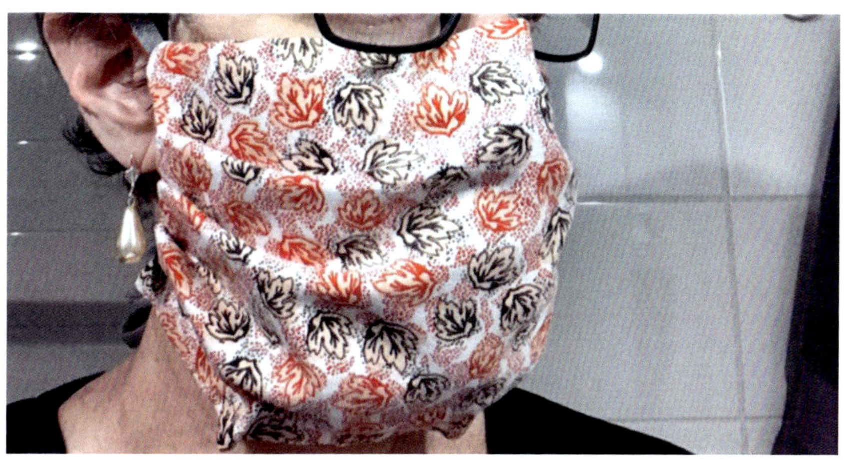

*Sunday, April 5*
Studies begin to show the inefficacy of ventilators in treating critically ill coronavirus patients.

*Monday, April 6*
New Mexico extends its stay-at-home order to April 30th.

> France: 98,010 cases; 8,911 deaths.
> US: 337,971 cases; 9,654 deaths.

*Tuesday April 7*
France imposes travel restrictions barring entry into France with exceptions for residents, workers, and the transport of goods. Travelers must now fill out an Exempted Movement Certificate before entering the country.

*Wednesday, April 8*
I pack again and, again, leave my groceries for the concierge.

I clap with my neighbors at 8 p.m.

I check-in for my flights.

> France: 110,070 cases; 10,869 deaths.
> Italy: 135,586 cases; 17,669 deaths.
> US: 392,594 cases; 12,621 deaths.

*Thursday, April 9*
I close the apartment, leaving a note on the ASUS laptop and its troublesome French keyboard, which I have returned to factory settings, saying that it is there for anyone to take.

I leave the key under the mat and wait on the street for Citizen Limousine.

The police are stopping all cars and checking papers.

The car arrives with the same driver as on March 26th. We both wear masks.

My last sunset in Paris (opposite page)

*Thursday, April 9, cont.*
I go to the gate. Every other seat in the waiting area is marked off for social distancing.

The captain comes out to the gate area. He gives a short speech about the difficulty of these times and how glad he is that he and the crew are able to help get us home. A crew member explains the new safety protocols.

When we land after the short flight, the captain welcomes us to Amsterdam, saying he hopes we meet again in better times. It is a surprisingly emotional moment.

It is a shock to see shops open in the Schiphol International Airport. I load up on souvenirs and buy myself a precious cup of coffee.

I walk through Amsterdam's large, nearly empty, airport. It is usually Europe's third busiest. Some passengers heading to Asia are in full hazmat suits.

The 737-800 to O'Hare starts to board. There are thirty-three passengers. The plane has 186 seats.

The KLM/Delta check-in at Charles de Gaulle

*Friday, April 10*
Paris extends its lockdown until May 11th.

The plane lands at O'Hare. I go through passport control. Temporary barriers are in place to guide us to the health screening tables where we have our temperatures taken. I drop off my destination address and contact information. No one collects my custom form.

I sleep for 24 hours straight.

> France: 125,930 cases; 8,598 deaths.
> US: over 500,000 cases; 18,693 deaths.
> The global death toll exceeds 100,000.

*April 10 through 24*
I quarantine in Naperville.

*Saturday, April 11*
France allows people to leave their homes in order to adopt pets as animal shelters are overflowing.

*Tuesday, April 14*
The Tour de France is delayed from June 27th to August 27th.

*Wednesday, April 15*
Emmanuel is rung at Notre Dame to commemorate the first anniversary of the 2019 fire.

*Friday, April 24*
The Paris Opera's costume shop starts to make masks for free distribution.

> France: 158,183 cases; 21,856 deaths.
> US: 886,709 cases; 50,243 deaths.

I pack again with a mask that Joan made me. Kurt drives me to O'Hare, and I fly nonstop to Denver on one of his standby passes.

O'Hare International Airport pedestrian tunnel
connecting United Airlines Terminals B & C

I arrive in Denver. My brother-in-law Steve picks me up.

Denver International Airport security check-in

*Friday, April 24 through May 1*
I stay in Denver and rest up for the drive back to Santa Fe.

*Tuesday, April 28*
US surpasses one million cases.

*Friday, May 1st*
I arrive back home in Santa Fe and begin two weeks of self-isolation.

> France: 128,121 cases; 24,342 deaths.
> US: 1,035,353 cases; 55,337 deaths.

*Mid-May*
Paris begins to slowly re-open.

*Thursday, May 21*
I correspond with Shakespeare and Co. about shipping a book of essays by Ursula K. Le Guin that I ordered from them pre-lockdown.

Their emails include a quote from her:

> Hard times are coming, when we'll be wanting the voices of writers who can see alternatives to how we live now, can see through our fear-stricken society . . . to other ways of being, and even imagine real grounds for hope . . ..

*Summer and Fall*
I continue to correspond with Shakespeare and Co. and order more books as they struggle to keep afloat during repeated lockdowns.

*Monday, September 28*
Global deaths surpass one million people.

*Monday, December 14*
The US begins Covid-19 vaccinations.

> France: 2,655,728 cases; 65,037 deaths.
> US: over 16 million cases; 299,193 deaths.

*Monday, December 28*
France begins Covid-19 vaccinations.

> France: 2,562,646 cases; 63,109 deaths.
> US: 20,640,214 cases; 351,590 deaths.

# Charts of COVID-19 Cases

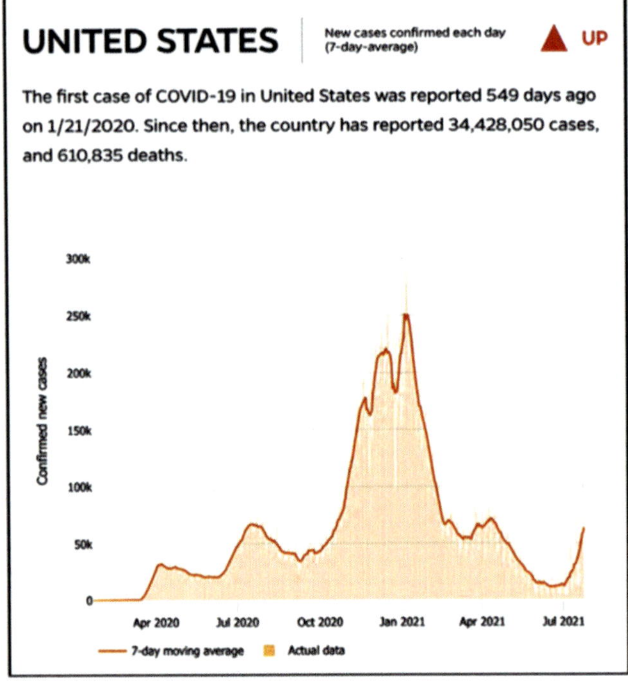



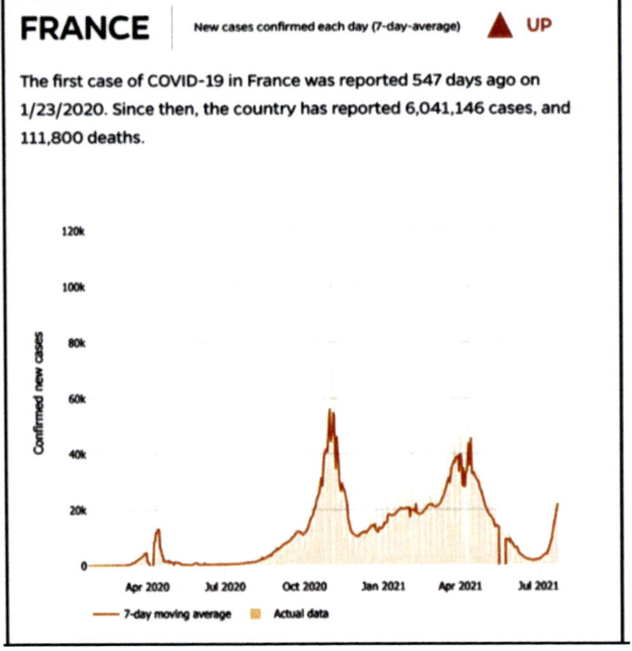



Source: Johns Hopkins University of Medicine, Coronavirus Research Center

# Epilogue

I have returned to Paris once since the first edition of this book was published in 2021. That was in 2023, during the post-Covid lockdown rush of "revenge" tourism, when tourists' pent-up frustrations of being forced to stay home exploded around the world.

I love Paris. I will always love Paris. But the Paris of 2023 was a new, not altogether happy, experience. Despite my best efforts, the tourists crowded out much of what I enjoy about Paris. Sauntering down the streets. Lingering in cafés. Wandering through museums. Browsing shopfront windows. Strolling through parks and gardens. There was still plenty to observe, but any musings were drowned out by the frenetic buzz of sightseers.

Some day I will return. I would like to see Notre Dame after the rebuilding is complete. I still haven't climbed to the top of the Arc de Triomphe or seen the view from Montparnasse Tower. Who knows? I may enroll in a French language class. Just kidding. But the Seine may be clean enough to swim in. There are more museums to explore and pastries to taste. And always, always, always cafés.

To be continued. . .

# Paris's Coat of Arms and Motto

Fluctuat nec mergitur.
"Tossed by the waves, she does not sink."

A mosaic in the métro

# Illustration Credits

Maps - France location map-Regions-2016.svg, by Superbenjamin, CC BY-SA 4.0 via Wikimedia Commons (author changed to B&W and added location names)

Maps - Paris arr jms-num.gif, by ThePromenader, user:yonidebest added the numbers, CC BY-SA 3.0  via Wikimedia Commons (author added location highlights)

p. 6 Plan metro Paris 2020.jpg, by Rayman78, CC BY-SA 4.0 via Wikimedia Commons

p. 14-15 Lutetia (51695980709).jpg, by Pierre (Rennes) from Rennes, FRANCE, CC BY-SA 2.0 via Wikimedia Commons

p. 16 National Archives at College Park, Public domain via Wikimedia Commons

p. 47 La Espadon Restaurant, The Ritz, Paris [unattributed]

p.47 Assainissement - Ville de Paris (postcard)

p. 49 from the brochure, Sewers . . . the underground Parisian point of view, The Paris Sewer System (July 2007) Creation T. Pierre - photos SAP/D.R.

p. 52 Rat silhouette created by Kevin US from The Noun Project

p. 53 Welsh Water, BBC News, Cardiff sewer fat weighing 800 tonnes removed (Dec. 29, 2018) https://www.bbc.com/news/uk-wales-46620603

p. 70 Published by Balades comtoises, Public domain

pp. 78-79 Pantheon_Paris.jpg, Author not set, CC BY-SA 3.0 via Wikimedia Commons

p. 81 Panthéon Pendule de Foucault2.JPG, by Rémih, CC BY-SA 3.0 via Wikimedia Commons

p. 83 reproduced with the kind permission of Benjamin Constable, http://benjamin-constable.net & https://www.coach-works.com

p. 99 Map of Paris-OSM 2020.png, Paris 16, CC BY-SA 4.0 via Wikimedia Commons (author cropped image and added triangle)

p. 124 Amtrak California Zephyr.jpg, by Jkan997, CC BY-SA 3.0 via Wikimedia Commons

p. 125 Amtrak Lake Shore Limited.svg, Author not set, CC BY-SA 4.0 via Wikimedia Commons

p. 136 Orion 3008 huge.jpg, by Mouser, CC BY-SA 3.0 via Wikimedia Commons

p. 139 National Geographic Society, Public domain via Wikimedia Commons

pp. 140-141 CIA, 2018, public domain

p. 154 Millennium Bridge (15668137242).jpg, by Tony Hisgett from Birmingham, UK, CC BY 2.0, via Wikimedia Commons

p. 155 St Paul's Cathedral High Altar, London, UK - Diliff.jpg, by Diliff, CC BY-SA 3.0 via Wikimedia Commons

p. 168 https://www.thamesclippers.com/plan-your-journey/route-map

p. 176 Thomas King. Portrait of John Harrison (1767)

p. 177 Prime Meridian Of The World (0° 0 0).jpg, by Andres Rueda, CC BY 2.0 via Wikimedia Commons

p. 178 Eurostar map.svg, by Rcsprinter123, CC BY 3.0 via Wikimedia Commons

p. 212 A Versailles, à Versailles 5 octobre 1789 - Restoration.jpg, Unknown artist; from Gallica Digital Library; available under the digital ID btv1b8410839z/f1 via Wikimedia Commons

p. 239 DictionaryFrenchAcademy1835.jpg, Académie française, Public domain via Wikimedia Commons

p. 246 Louvre Map, https://ontheworldmap.com/france/city/paris/louvre-map.html

Throughout: Photos of Paris by Carol L. Couch, Jeanne Daill, and Joan Julian

All other photos: Carol L. Couch

# Acknowledgements

This book was not a solo project.

My dear friends Lynn Pickard and Gina Maestas, colleagues from the New Mexico Court of Appeals and travel buddies, shared in my first and many subsequent Paris adventures. Without them, I would never have indulged in my passion for the City of Lights.

Joan Julian volunteered her considerable design talents to transform a clunky manuscript into the elegant, stylish book you have before you. This was no small task.

Jeanne Daill reworked old digital images to render them fit for publication.

Barbara Hopkins believed in the value of this book and encouraged me to send it out into the world. She and her husband Steve provided my launching pad for repeated trips to Paris and gave me much peace of mind as they cared for my sweet kitty Sabina.

And my son Zachary, who, simply by his existence, makes me want to be the best person I can be.

To these and all the other kind and generous people who provided support and feedback, thank you.

# About the Author

A writer and coffee addict, Carol Couch lives in Santa Fe, New Mexico. With a BA in English Literature and a JD from Notre Dame Law School, she spent her career writing for the New Mexico Court of Appeals. Her pilgrimages to Paris prompted a desire to stretch beyond the legal realm and share her thoughts and experiences in more playful prose.

You can usually find her in the nearest café, watching the world and wondering what it all means.